Open Learning

WordPerfect

Version 5.1 for DOS and Windows

Open Learning

WordPerfect

Version 5.1 for DOS and Windows

G G Skinner & E M Prentice

Pitman Publishing

PITMAN PUBLISHING
128 Long Acre, London, WC2E 9AN
A Division of Longman Group UK Limited

First published in Great Britain 1993

British Library Cataloguing-in-Publication Data

A catalogue record for this book is available
from the British Library

ISBN 0 273 03808 7

Printed and bound in Great Britain

Acknowledgements

WordPerfect is a registered trademark of WordPerfect Corporation.
MS-DOS and Windows are registered trademarks of Microsoft Corporation.
IBM is a registered trademark of International Business Machines Corporation.

Contents

Introduction

Overview

WordPerfect version 5.1 is a word processing package which runs on an IBM PC-compatible microcomputer. It is available in two versions, one which will work on almost any PC; the other, *WordPerfect for Windows* requires Microsoft Windows (version 3.0 at least) to be installed on your machine.

Using this book

This book is intended for the use of anyone who wishes to learn WordPerfect version 5.1 for DOS or Windows, with little or no additional support. Each unit can be used independently, so that you can practise any particular aspect of the software without necessarily working through all the units which precede it.

Most of the activities are based on realistic business documents so that you will learn the standard layout and design of these documents while acquiring operating knowledge and skills.

Each free-standing unit consists of existing skills, some new skills, activities and instructions. Once you have read and understood each group of instructions, you will be able to undertake the activity which goes with them. The units also contain suggestions for further use of the techniques included, and solutions to the problems which you may encounter.

If you want to use a particular unit, then you should first check that you have already mastered the existing skills you need for it.

Unit X

Overview

Existing skills

New skills

Numbered instructions

Activities

Further uses

Problem solving

Operation

WordPerfect for Windows is operated through menus which are selected with a mouse pointer. The DOS version can be operated through on-screen menus, accessed in one of two ways:

• **Mouse and pointer**

If you have a mouse fitted, then you can point at one of the options on the menu bar at the top of the screen and click the left mouse button. The appropriate pull-down menu will be displayed. You can then make selections from the menu by pointing at the option and clicking the mouse button.

• **Alt key and letters**

If you have no mouse then you can access the menus by *tapping* the **Alt** key, at the left-hand side of the space bar on your keyboard, to highlight the first option on the menu bar, **File**. You can then pull-down any menu, using the highlighted letter for each, ie

F - File	E - Edit
S - Search	L - Layout
M - Mark	T - Tools
O - Font	G - Graphics

Once a pull-down menu is displayed, you can select an option by typing its highlighted letter, or highlighting it with the cursor (using the cursor control arrow keys) and pressing **Return**.

Using keys

Function keys

The function keys should be found above or to the left of the main keyboard, marked F1 to F10, or F12, depending on your keyboard. The function of each key is displayed on the keystrip provided with the WordPerfect package. A table for function key use is included as an appendix.

Exit key

The function key **F7** is used throughout WordPerfect for DOS as an EXIT key from the current mode, menu or screen.

Alt key

The Alt (Alternate) key is used to access the menus in the DOS version, if you have no mouse installed.

Shift key If the Shift key is held down and used with any of the alphabetic keys, this will give you upper case, in the same way as a conventional typewriter. It can also be used in conjuction with the function keys (like Ctrl and Alt).

Caps lock If you need a number of characters in upper case, pressing the Caps lock key on will enable you to type them without having to hold down the Shift key.

Return key The Return key is used to complete a menu entry as well as to move the cursor to a new line. The Enter key on the numeric keypad is identical in effect and can be used interchangeably with it.

Delete key This key will erase the character at the cursor position when pressed; if held down it will automatically carry on erasing.

Backspace key The Backspace delete key will erase the character immediately to the left of the cursor position; if held down it will automatically carry on erasing.

Insert key The Insert key, when pressed, selects *Insert mode* (you can insert additional text without affecting what is there already) and *Overstrike mode* (text typed replaces existing text).

Cursor keys The cursor keys on the numeric keypad to the right of the main keyboard (and repeated between the numeric and main keyboards on an extended keyboard) move the cursor position in the direction indicated. They are also used to move the cursor in menus.

Version differences

Although the DOS and Windows versions of WordPerfect 5.1 are very similar, there are a few differences between versions in the menu options offered. Those listed below are the ones which affect the activities included in the units following. The instructions in the study units are written for the DOS version. However, you will find that you can identify the options you want in the Windows version quite easily using the menu bar and buttons, as shown overleaf.

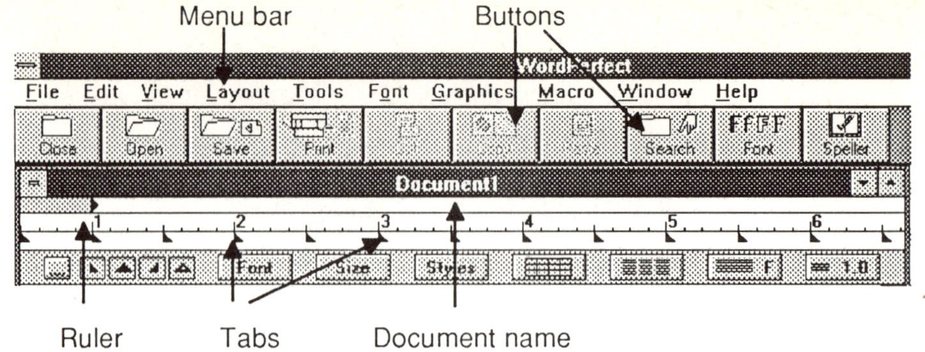

The main differences between versions are not in their operation, but in the exact menu option used, especially in the File and Layout menus.

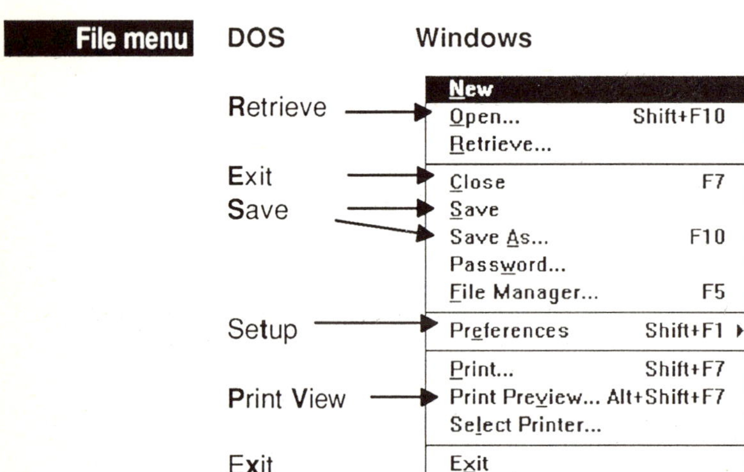

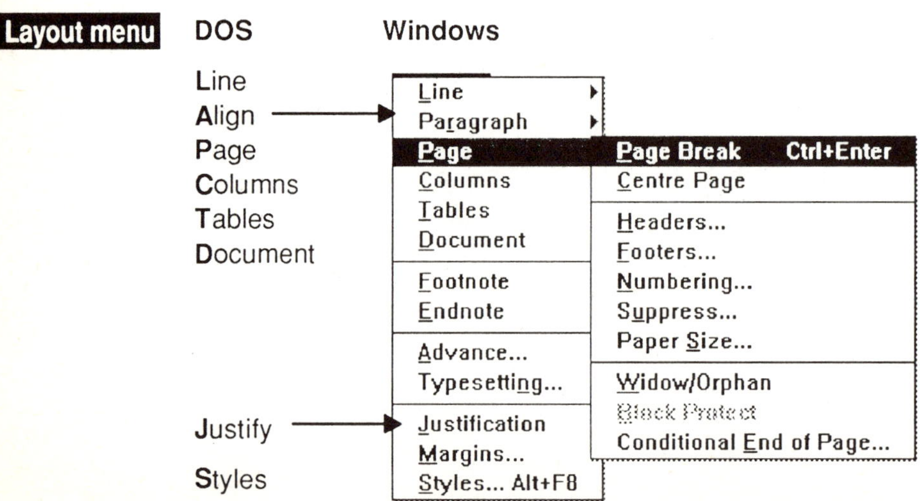

Preparing to use WordPerfect

Overview WordPerfect is a very powerful word processing program, which is capable of being set up to work in a number of different ways. Before you use units 1 - 21, you need to set up WordPerfect in a way which will make it easier for you to use the material.

All you have to do is to follow the procedure given in this unit very carefully. It is not necessary to understand all the steps you are taking. Most of them will become clear to you as you work through the material.

Important

1 If you have any problems in your preparation, then the best thing to do is to ask a more experienced friend to do it for you.

2 Throughout this material, it is assumed that you are using a machine which has a **hard disk** fitted on which WordPerfect 5.1 has been installed. The DOS version of WordPerfect can be used on a twin floppy machine (where WordPerfect 5.1 must be loaded from disk each time the computer is turned on), but this is not advisable; there are less powerful programs on the market which are much more suitable for this type of machine. Alternatively, a hard disk upgrade is not expensive.

1 Installation

DOS version

1 Check that you have at least 3 Mb of free space on your hard disk.

2 Follow the instructions to install WordPerfect given on the Installation card, accepting any defaults given to you about disk drives and directories. WordPerfect will be installed in the newly created directory **C:\WP51**.

Windows

1 Check that Windows version 3 or higher is installed on your machine and that you have at least 6 Mb of free space on your hard disk, ideally 9 Mb.

2 Follow the instructions to install WordPerfect for Windows given on page 5 of the Reference manual provided with the software, accepting any options given to you about disk drives and directories.

3 When you are given a choice of keyboards, choose the WordPerfect keyboard. This makes operation very similar to the DOS version.

2 Loading WordPerfect

DOS version

1 Turn on your machine and wait for it to start up.

2 With the DOS prompt **C:** on screen, type **CD \WP51** and press **Return**.

3 Type **WP** and press **Return**. Lower or upper case letters can be used.

4 The WordPerfect screen will be displayed.

Windows

1 Start up Windows to display the Program Manager screen.

2 Click the mouse when the screen arrow is on the WordPerfect window which will have been set up by the installation program.

3 Double click on the WordPerfect icon to load up.

4 The WordPerfect screen will be displayed.

3 Displaying menus

DOS version

The defaults which are set for WordPerfect 5.1 for DOS are chosen to make it compatible with previous versions, so that current users find the transition easier. New users, however, will wish to opt for more usual settings to help ease of access, using menus on screen rather than function keys. The menu bar, for example, may be set to permanent display.

1 Hold down Shift and tap function key **F1** to display the **Setup** menu.

2 Press **D** to select the **Display** menu, then press **M** to select **Menu Options** to display the possible choices for menu display.

```
Setup:
  1 - Mouse
  2 - Display
  3 - Environment
  4 - Initial Settings
  5 - Keyboard Layout
  6 - Location of Files
```

```
Setup: Display
  1 - Colour/Fonts/Attributes
  2 - Graphics Screen Type
  3 - Text Screen Type
  4 - Menu Options
  5 - View-Document Options
  6 - Edit-Screen Options
```

3 The Menu Options screen has choices as shown below. **4 7 8** will probably all be set to **No.** Choose each in turn, by pressing the appropriate number or letter and press **Y** to make sure the menu bar is displayed and you can access it. After this the selections shown should be displayed.

```
Setup: Menu Options
  1 - Menu Letter Display                 BOLD
Pull-Down Menus
  2 - Pull-Down Letter Display
  3 - Pull-Down Text
  4 - Alt Key Selects Pull-Down Menu      Yes
Menu Bar
  5 - Menu-Bar Letter Display
  6 - Menu-Bar Text
  7 - Menu-Bar Separator Line             Yes
  8 - Menu-Bar Remains Visible            Yes
```

4 Press function key **F7** to confirm your choices.

5 Then select **Edit-Screen Options** from the **Setup: Display** screen and select **Hard Return Display Character.** Press a cursor key to set the return character to be a reverse block.

6 Press **F7** to confirm and return to the main screen. The menus should now be displayed.

Windows Menus are already set in the Windows version, as they are an integral part of Windows. No action is required.

4 Changing colours

You should need to change the default screen colours only if you are using a monochrome screen. The colours chosen may not give sufficient contrast. For example, the default colour for underlining in the DOS version is unsuitable for monochrome screens.

DOS version

1 Select **Setup** from the **File** menu, followed by **Display** and **Colour/Fonts/Attributes**.

2 Select **Screen Colours** for Underlining. Choosing colours **B** for Foreground and **H** for Background will give a reasonable level of contrast.

3 Make any other changes you think desirable. Each will be shown on screen as a sample, as you make your selections.

4 Press function key **F7** to return to your text screen.

Windows

The only colour which seems to cause a problem is the one used for codes when you Reveal Codes, so it is worth changing this.

1 Select **Preferences** from the **File** menu, followed by **Display** to show the **Display Settings** dialog box.

2 Click on the **Reveal Codes Colours** box at the bottom of the dialog box.

3 Click on **Codes**, the centre button and then select the black box in the Background Palette, to show how the codes will now be shown.

4 Click on **OK** in that box and the next one displayed to display the text.

5 Setting default paper size

This is only necessary if you are using the DOS version of WordPerfect, as you can choose to use a Windows printer for the Windows version.

DOS version

1 Select **Setup** from the **File** menu, followed by **Initial Settings**.

2 Select **5** or Initial **C**odes, to display the hidden initial codes in your file.

3 Use the cursor to highlight and delete the code for Paper size.

4 Select **Page** from the **Layout** menu to display the **Format: Page** menu.

5 Choose **Paper Size/Type**, highlight the paper size required and choose **1** or **S**elect. This will be either 11" continuous, or A4 single sheet.

6 Press function key **F7** to return to the text screen.

Unit 1

Text entry

Overview When word processing, you can type continuously, without worrying about line endings, margins, tabs, pagination and so on. All these can be set later, if you do not want to use the default settings.

New skills

- Keying in text
- Using Backspace delete to correct mistakes as you type
- Saving text to disk
- Printing text

Important You do not press the Return (Enter) key at the end of each line, only at the end of a paragraph or after a heading. (In the sample below ↵ stands for Return.)

```
Word Processing↵
↵
Word processing is the processing of text to produce typed
work by computer. Its applications include producing
documentation of all types and editing text which is
particularly useful for reports and minutes.↵
↵
You only press Return at the end of a paragraph, or to
make a blank line after a heading or between paragraphs.
In all other cases, the word processing package will
organise the text on to lines.↵
↵
You will see the cursor move to the next line as you key.↵
```

1.1 Typing text in a new file

1 Load up WordPerfect to display a blank screen. The cursor, a flashing underline, is at the top left of the screen, just below the menu bar. This marks the position where text you type will be displayed.

2 Key in the text, pressing the space bar once at the end of each word and after commas, full stops, or any other punctuation. The cursor will move as you type.

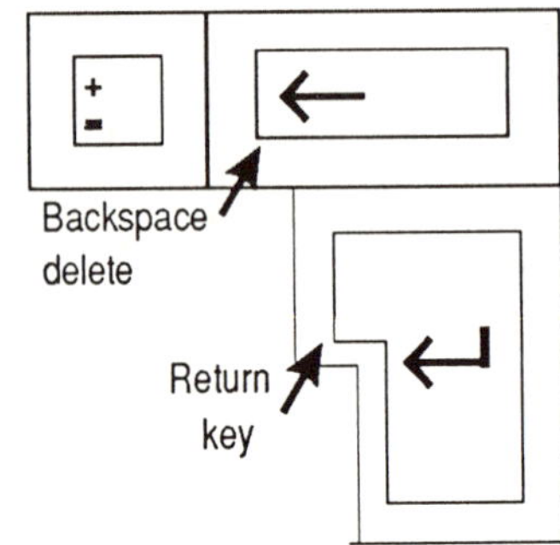

3 If you type an incorrect character, use the **Backspace** delete key to move the cursor back over it and delete it.

4 Press the **Return** key *only*

- at the end of paragraphs
- after a heading
- for a blank line after headings/paragraphs

Activity 1

1 Load up WordPerfect
2 Type in the following heading and paragraph, pressing **Return** twice at the end of the heading and once at the end of the paragraph
3 Use the Backspace key to delete any characters you key wrongly

```
WORD PROCESSING

Word processing has steadily increased in popularity since
the early 1970s. Operators have been delighted with the
ease of keyboarding and the facilities for correction and
editing. Repetitive typing has become a thing of the past
and all work can be produced to a very high standard.
```

1.2 Saving new text to disk

1 Select **Save** from the **File** menu.

2 The message *Document to be saved:* will be displayed at the bottom of the screen.

3 Key in your selected file name (up to 8 letters or digits, followed by a full stop and up to 3 letters or digits), and press **Return**.

4 The disk light will flash very quickly as the file is saved and then the file name will be displayed at the bottom of the screen.

1.3 Printing the text on screen

Important Before you print, you should make the following checks to your printer. It should be:

- switched on
- on-line
- loaded with paper

1 With your text displayed on screen, select **Print** from the **File** menu to display the Printing screen.

```
Print
1 - Full Document
2 - Page
3 - Document on Disk
4 - Control Printer
5 - Multiple Pages
6 - New Document
7 - View Document
8 - Initialise Printer

S - Select Printer                         Printer name
B - Binding Offset                         0"
N - Number of Copies                       1
M - Multiple Copies Generated by           WordPerfect
G - Graphics Quality                       Medium
T - Text Quality                           High
```

2 Check your printer and select **1** or **F**ull Document from the menu.

3 Your text will be printed.

4 Reload the printer with paper, if necessary.

Activity 2

1 Save the paragraph of text you have just entered with the name **UNIT1-1**
2 Print the text which is still on screen

1.4 Clearing text from the screen

1 Select **Exit** from the **File** menu. The message *Save document? **Y**es (**N**o)* will be displayed at the bottom of the screen.

2 If you have already saved the text on screen, select **N**o.

3 The message *Exit WordPerfect? **N**o (**Y**es)* will be displayed at the bottom of the screen.

4 If you want to do some more word processing, select **N**o.

1.5 Retrieving text from disk

1 Save any text which is on screen, if you have not already done so, and clear the screen.

2 Select **Retrieve** from the **File** menu.

3 The message *Document to be retrieved:* will be displayed at the bottom of the screen.

4 Key in the name of the file you want to retrieve and press **Return**.

5 The file will be displayed on screen.

1.6 Listing files for retrieval

If you have forgotten the name of the file you want, you can display the name of all the files on your disk on screen.

1 Select **List Files** from the **File** menu.

2 The name of the current directory *C:\WP51*.** and the message (*Type = to change default Dir*) will be displayed across the bottom of the screen.

3 When the correct drive is displayed, press **Return**. All those files contained on the disk in the selected drive will be displayed.

4 Highlight the name of the file you want and select **1** or **R**etrieve from the menu at the foot of the screen.

5 Your file will be displayed on screen for editing.

1.7 Adding to existing text

1 Retrieve the existing file, if it is not already on screen.

2 Move your cursor to the end of the text and, if a blank line is needed to separate the new text from the old, press **Return**.

3 Key in the additional text, using Backspace to delete any mistakes.

1.8 Saving existing text to disk

1 When you have made any additions or corrections to the text, select **Save** from the **File** menu.

2 The message *Document to be saved: C:\WP51\xxxxx* with xxxxx replaced by the file name of your existing text, will appear on screen.

3 Press **Return** to confirm the file name.

4 The message *Replace C:\WP51\xxxxx?* **N***o (*Y*es) will be displayed.*

5 Select **Y**es to save the file with the same name.

Activity 3

1 Clear the text to display the typing screen
2 Retrieve the file **UNIT1-1** and add, at the end, the 2 paragraphs shown below
3 Save the text again with the same name

```
Other useful software is a Thesaurus and there are even
programs to pick up grammatical mistakes.

Word processing is very popular with home users and the
cost of the machines has dropped so dramatically during
recent years, that they have become within the reach of
many users who had previously been content with a manual,
electric or electronic typewriter.
```

1.9 Printing text from disk

1 Select **Print** from the **File** menu.

2 Select **3** or **D**ocument on disk from the Printing screen.

3 The message *Document name:* will be displayed at the bottom of the screen. Type in the name of the file to be printed and press **Return**.

4 At the message *Page(s): (All)* press **Return** to confirm.

Activity 4

1 Make sure that you have saved the **UNIT1-1** with the extra text you added in Activity 3
2 Clear the screen
3 Print the complete file **UNIT1-1** from disk, which should look like the example given below

```
WORD PROCESSING

Word processing has steadily increased in popularity since
the early 1970s.  Operators have been delighted with the
ease of keyboarding and the facilities for correction and
editing.  Repetitive typing has become a thing of the past
and all work can be produced to a very high standard.

Other useful software is a Thesaurus and there are even
programs to pick up grammatical mistakes.

Word processing is very popular with home users and the
cost of the machines has dropped so dramatically during
recent years, that they have become within the reach of
many users who had previously been content with a manual,
electric or electronic typewriter.
```

Activity 5

1 Clear the screen if necessary
2 Key in the text given below, using Return twice at the end of each heading and once at the end of each paragraph
3 Save the text with the file name **UNIT1-2**

```
WP OPERATORS

When operating a WP for any length of time it is important
to ensure that working conditions are comfortable.  If a
few simple precautions are not observed, the work can lead
to headaches and backaches.

THE VDU

The VDU should be sited so that there is no reflection on
the screen, which could cause eye-strain.
```

Activity 6

1 Retrieve the file **UNIT1-2**, if necessary
2 Add to the text the additional third heading and paragraph shown below
3 Re-save the file with the same name
4 Print the file, so that you have a paper copy

```
WP OPERATORS

When operating a WP for any length of time it is important
to ensure that working conditions are comfortable.  If a
few simple precautions are not observed, the work can lead
to headaches and backaches.

THE VDU

The VDU should be sited so that there is no reflection on
the screen, which could cause eye-strain.

DESK AND CHAIR

The workstation or desk should be at a comfortable height
for the operator and an adjustable chair should be used so
that the back is supported at all times whilst the feet
are flat on the floor.
```

Further uses

1 Producing letters and reports

2 Saving text for later use

3 Producing several copies of text

Problem solving

- *The message "File not found" is displayed when you have typed in your file name to save the text.*

  You used invalid characters in your file name. You can use only letters, digits and the hyphen (not as the first character). Save again, and use the file name suggested.

- *Your Print command does not work.*

  The printer may have no paper, or be switched off, or not be on-line. Go to the Print screen and select **4** or **C**ontrol Printer. The Control Printer screen will give you hints on the problem you have. Select **1** or **C**ancel Job(s) to stop printing and then go through the printing routine again.

- *You cannot find your file on the disk.*

  You may have typed the name UNIT followed by space. As spaces are not allowed in file names, the file will have been stored as UNIT. Try retrieving this instead. If this is not successful, select **List Files** from the File menu and search for it. It should have today's date.

- *The document you have retrieved is mixed up on screen with one you already had on screen.*

  You did not clear the screen before you retrieved a file from disk. Clear the screen now and then retrieve the new file again.

- *The cursor will not move within the text of a file just retrieved from disk.*

  You have probably highlighted a file for retrieval when using the **List Files** command and then pressed **Return**, instead of selecting **Retrieve**. Press the Escape key to return to the file listing and select the file again.

- *Your paragraphs are not in the correct order in one of your documents.*

  The cursor was not at the end of the existing text when you keyed in the extra texts. Delete the new text, move the cursor to the end and key the text in again.

- *There is not a blank line between each paragraph.*

  You did not press **Return** to add a blank line before you added text. Position the cursor on the first letter of the paragraph with no blank line before it and press **Return** to insert a blank line.

Unit 2

Text editing

Overview

One of the main advantages of word processing is that it saves you from having to rekey text which you have used before; blocks of text can be repeated automatically. You can retrieve your text from disk and make any changes you like. You can even find spelling mistakes and mistypes and correct them automatically.

Existing skills

- Keying in text - Unit 1
- Retrieving text from disk - Unit 1
- Saving and printing text - Unit 1

New skills

- Inserting extra text
- Deleting unwanted text
- Rearranging text
- Copying blocks of text
- Checking spelling

Important Should you change your mind immediately after you have deleted text, you may reverse the process and reinstate the deleted text using the **Undelete** command.

2.1 Inserting text

When you use WordPerfect, the setting Insert mode is **on** by default. This means that as new characters are keyed, the existing text moves to accommodate them.

1 Move your cursor to the point in the existing text where the additional character is to be inserted.

2 Key in the characters which are to be inserted.

Important You can insert Spaces and Returns, as well as ordinary characters like A and D. This will often be necessary to make blank lines and to separate words.

Activity 1

1 If you have already completed Unit 1 and so have **UNIT1-1** saved to disk, retrieve it and display it on screen
or
If this file is not on disk, key in the heading and first three paragraphs given below, beginning each line at the left hand margin and leaving one clear line after the heading and each paragraph
2 Insert the additional paragraph shown at the end, in the position indicated by the arrow
3 Save with the same name as before

```
WORD PROCESSING

Word processing has steadily increased in popularity since
the early 1970s.  Operators have been delighted with the
ease of keyboarding and the facilities for correction and
editing.  Repetitive typing has become a thing of the past
and all work can be produced to a very high standard.

Other useful software is a Thesaurus and there are even
programs to pick up grammatical mistakes.

Word processing is very popular with home users and the
cost of the machines has dropped so dramatically during
recent years, that they have become within the reach of
many users who had previously been content with a manual,
electric or electronic typewriter.

Even if you are not familiar with the keyboard, you can
still use a word processor to good advantage because of
the ease of correction.  Many operators use a spelling
check program to aid in proofreading their work.  Although
a checker will not pick up such mistakes as 'know' for
'now', it will identify many mistypes.
```

2.2 Deleting a character

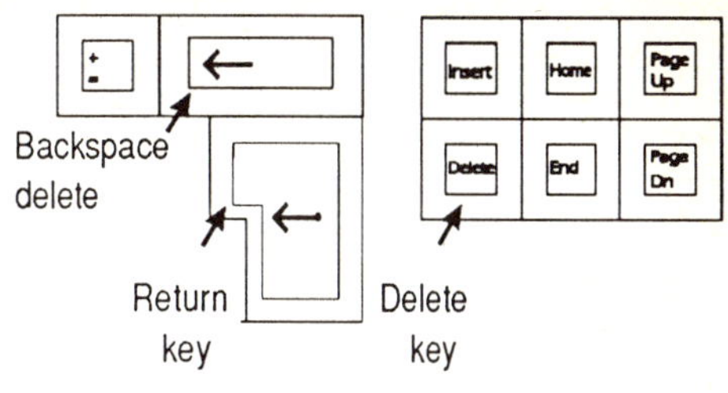

If you have completed Unit 1, you have already used the Backspace delete, which moves the cursor to the left, deleting as it moves. The Delete key, shown in the diagram deletes the character at the cursor position, rather than one to the left.

1 Move the cursor to the character to be deleted.

2 Press the Delete key once. Repeat this process to delete more text.

Important

You can delete Spaces and Returns, as well as ordinary characters like A and D. This will often be necessary to remove blank lines and any extra spaces.

Activity 2

1 Retrieve the file **UNIT1-1**, if it is not already on screen
2 Delete the third paragraph, as marked below
3 Save the new version with the same name and print a copy

```
WORD PROCESSING

Word processing has steadily increased in popularity since
the early 1970s.  Operators have been delighted with the
ease of keyboarding and the facilities for correction and
editing.  Repetitive typing has become a thing of the past
and all work can be produced to a very high standard.

Even if you are not familiar with the keyboard, you can
still use a word processor to good advantage because of
the ease of correction.  Many operators use a spelling
check program to aid in proofreading their work.  Although
a checker will not pick up such mistakes as 'know' for
'now', it will identify many mistypes.

Other useful software is a Thesaurus and there are even
programs to pick up grammatical mistakes.

Word processing is very popular with home users and the
cost of the machines has dropped so dramatically during
recent years, that they have become within the reach of
many users who had previously been content with a manual,
electric or electronic typewriter.
```

2.3 Cutting and pasting text

Text can be highlighted, marked as a block and manipulated as a single item.

1 Highlight the text with your mouse, by pointing at the first character, pressing the left mouse button and dragging to the end of the text.
or
With the cursor at the first character, select **Block** from the **Edit** menu and then move the cursor to highlight the complete piece of text.

2 Select **Move (Cut)** from the **Edit** menu. The highlighted block will disappear from screen. It has been saved temporarily.

3 Move your cursor to the new position for the block and select **Paste** from the **Edit** menu.

4 Select **1** or **B**lock from the menu at the bottom of the screen. The marked block will be inserted into your text at the cursor.

Activity 3

1 If you have already completed Unit 1 and so have **UNIT1-2** saved to disk, retrieve it and display it on screen
or
If this file is not on disk, key in the headings and paragraphs given below, beginning each line at the left hand margin and leaving one clear line after each heading and paragraph

2 Move the last heading and paragraph as indicated below, deleting and inserting Returns, as required, to give the correct display

3 Save the new version and print, if required

```
WP OPERATORS

When operating a WP for any length of time it is important
to ensure that working conditions are comfortable.  If a
few simple precautions are not observed, the work can lead
to headaches and backaches.

THE VDU

The VDU should be sited so that there is no reflection on
the screen, which could cause eyestrain.

DESK AND CHAIR

The workstation or desk should be at a comfortable height
for the operator and an adjustable chair should be used so
that the back is supported at all times whilst the feet
are flat on the floor.
```

2.4 Deleting blocks of text

There is a method by which you can delete a whole piece of text at once, rather than by repeatedly using the Backspace or Delete keys, which is slow and can be inaccurate.

1 Mark the text as a block, as before.

2 Press the Delete key. The message *Delete Block?* ***No*** *(Yes)* will be displayed at the foot of the screen.

3 Select **Yes** to delete the text.

2.5 Undeleting text

1 Immediately you have deleted a character or a marked block of text, select **Undelete** from the **Edit** menu.

2 The deleted text will be replaced in the same position.

Important Undeleting works only immediately after a deletion, and then only for one character if you have deleted with the Backspace delete or Delete keys.

Activity 4

1 Retrieve the file **UNIT1-2**, if it is not already on screen
2 Delete the second paragraph, using the block method
3 Use undelete to replace the text

```
WP OPERATORS

When operating a WP for any length of time it is important
to ensure that working conditions are comfortable.  If a
few simple precautions are not observed, the work can lead
to headaches and backaches.

DESK AND CHAIR

The workstation or desk should be at a comfortable height
for the operator and an adjustable chair should be used so
that the back is supported at all times whilst the feet
are flat on the floor.

THE VDU

The VDU should be sited so that there is no reflection on
the screen, which could cause eyestrain.
```

Activity 5

1 Retrieve the file **UNIT1-1**
2 Cut the last paragraph and paste it in, as shown
3 Save and print, if required

```
WORD PROCESSING

Word processing has steadily increased in popularity since
the early 1970s.  Operators have been delighted with the
ease of keyboarding and the facilities for correction and
editing.  Repetitive typing has become a thing of the past
and all work can be produced to a very high standard.

Even if you are not familiar with the keyboard, you can
still use a word processor to good advantage because of
the ease of correction.  Many operators use a spelling
check program to aid in proofreading their work.  Although
a checker will not pick up such mistakes as 'know' for
'now', it will identify many mistypes.

Word processing is very popular with home users and the
cost of the machines has dropped so dramatically during
recent years, that they have become within the reach of
many users who had previously been content with a manual,
electric or electronic typewriter.
```

2.6 Copying blocks of text

You can save a considerable amount of keying time by copying blocks of text which are needed in several places.

1 Mark the text as a block, as before.

2 Select **Copy** from the **Edit** menu. The message *Move cursor; press* ***Enter*** *to retrieve* will appear.

3 Move the cursor to the position in the text where the second copy is to appear and press **Return**. The text will appear on screen.

2.7 Checking spelling

1 Select **Spell** from the **Tools** menu.

2 Select **3** or **D**ocument from the options displayed at the foot of the screen, to check spelling throughout the file.

3 Each word not found in the dictionary will be highlighted in turn. You can make the following choices about the word:

`1 Skip Once; 2 Skip; 3 Add; 4 Edit; 5 Look Up; 6 Ignore Numbers`

4 For any word which is not a real mis-spelling, perhaps a name which will not be in the dictionary, you can Skip. You can Add any special words for your area of interest to a personal dictionary.

5 Select the correct word from the suggestions listed on screen for real mistypes or misspellings. If you have so mistyped the word that it bears no resemblance to the word intended, there may be no suggestions which are correct, and you will have to select Edit to correct the word manually.

Activity 5

1 Clear the screen, if necessary
2 Key in the following notice for display in newsagents' windows
3 Use the spell checker to correct the common spelling mistakes made in it
4 Mark and copy the whole notice, so that it fits 3 times on a sheet of A4 paper, leaving several blank lines between copies, for cutting
5 Save as file **UNIT2-1** and print a copy

```
ACCOMODATION WANTED

Mature student, clean, non-smoker, requires furnished room
with shared facilitys from September, in Bridgford area.

Serius replies only, please, to Alex on 818818 (daytime
only before 5 pm).

Good refferences supplied.



ACCOMODATION WANTED

Mature student, clean, non-smoker, requires furnished room
with shared facilitys from September, in Bridgford area.

Serius replies only, please, to Alex on 818818 (daytime
```
etc

Further uses

1 Redrafting reports and minutes

2 Using similar pieces of text to produce new ones

3 Checking spelling in initial proofreading

Problem solving

- *When you try to insert text, the existing text is deleted and replaced by the new text you are keying in.*

  You have probably pressed the Insert key by mistake, which switches word processing into Typeover mode, ie keying in replaces text, rather than inserting as usual. If you have, the word **Typeover** will be displayed at the bottom left hand side of the screen. Press the Insert key again, to reverse this and rekey the letters you have deleted.

- *The text you retrieved is not what you wanted.*

  Either you typed in the wrong file name, or you highlighted the wrong file name when Listing files, or you saved the file with the wrong name. List Files, highlight each file with the correct date, and press Return to display it on screen. Press **F7** to go back to the list of files. Repeat this process until you find the text you want. Highlight it and select **Retrieve**.

- *You cannot remember the name of the file you want.*

  List files and look through the names, searching for ones with the appropriate date and time when you last used the file.

- *There is no blank line between two paragraphs, but more than one between others.*

  You did not include the blank line in your block when you highlighted. Position the cursor on the first letter of the paragraph with no blank line before it and press Return to insert a blank line. Then position the cursor on the first line of the paragraph with more than one blank line and press Backspace delete to get rid of a blank line. Repeat, if necessary.

- *Your paragraphs are in a different order from the sample given.*

  Your cursor was in the wrong position when you moved or copied a block of text. Select the block again and move it again, making sure to position the cursor correctly before completing the move or copy.

- *You have chosen the wrong word to replace a spelling mistake.*

  Position the cursor at the beginning of the word, use the Delete key to delete it and key in the correct word.

Unit 3

Headings

Overview Headings can be emphasised in a number of different ways, to make them stand out from ordinary text. The most commonly used methods are to centre, underline or embolden the text.

Existing skills

- Entering and editing text - Units 1 and 2
- Saving and retrieving files - Units 1 and 2

New skills

- Centring text on a line
- Enhancing text - using special features for emphasis eg emboldening, underlining, italics

Important Emboldening and centring are examples of the few operations best carried out using function keys, rather than menu options, as this is much faster.

Most enhancements are not shown on screen, but you can choose colours to display each of them if you have a colour screen. On a monochrome screen, you can choose reverse (black text on white), or bright or dim text.

FUNCTION	EXAMPLE	COMMAND TO BEGIN AND END
Bold	**Enhanced**	**F6**
Underline	Enhanced	**F8**
Italics	*Enhanced*	**F**ont **A**ppearance **I**talics
Double underline	Enhanced	**F**ont **A**ppearance **O**utline
Strikeout	~~Enhanced~~	**F**ont **A**ppearance **S**trikeout

3.1 Centring existing text

Headings can be centred to give attractive display. Centring is shown on screen.

1 Key in the text, starting each line at the left margin.

2 Move your cursor to the beginning of the line to be centred and select **Align** from the **Layout** menu.

3 Select **Centre**. Your text will again be displayed on screen.

4 Move the cursor down to the next line. The line will be centred on screen.

5 Follow the same procedure for each line to be centred.

Activity 1

1 If you have already completed Unit 2 and so have **UNIT1-2** saved to disk, retrieve it and display it on screen
or
If the file is not on disk, key in the text given below, beginning each line at the left margin and leaving one clear line after each heading and paragraph

2 Centre each heading line

3 Save the text with filename **UNIT3-1** and print one copy

```
WP OPERATORS

When operating a WP for any length of time it is important
to ensure that working conditions are comfortable.  If a
few simple precautions are not observed, the work can lead
to headaches and backaches.

DESK AND CHAIR

The workstation or desk should be at a comfortable height
for the operator and an adjustable chair should be used so
that the back is supported at all times whilst the feet
are flat on the floor.

THE VDU

The VDU should be sited so that there is no reflection on
the screen, which could cause eyestrain.
```

3.2 Centring while keying in

1 When you reach a line which is to be centred, position the cursor at the beginning of the line.

2 Select **Align** from the **Layout** menu.

3 Select **Centre** and then enter the text for the line. The text will be entered at the centre of the line.

4 Press **Return** at the end of the line to end centred entry.

Activity 2

1 Retrieve the file **UNIT3-1**, if it is not already on screen
2 Enter the additional heading, centring it before entry
3 Add the extra paragraph, as shown
4 Proofread the text on screen and make any changes necessary
5 Save the file again and print a revised copy

WP OPERATORS

When operating a WP for any length of time it is important to ensure that working conditions are comfortable. If a few simple precautions are not observed, the work can lead to headaches and backaches.

DESK AND CHAIR

The workstation or desk should be at a comfortable height for the operator and an adjustable chair should be used so that the back is supported at all times whilst the feet are flat on the floor.

THE VDU

The VDU should be sited so that there is no reflection on the screen, which could cause eyestrain.

BREAKS

Breaks are important and an operator would be well advised not to work more than 2 hours at a VDU without a break.

3.3 Enhancing existing text

Enhancing *existing* text is achieved by highlighting the text to be enhanced with the cursor or mouse and then applying the enhancement. Underlining, emboldening, double underlining, italics and a host of other special effects are available, limited only by your printer.

1. Select the text to be enhanced with the mouse, or move your cursor to the first letter of the text, select **Block** from the **Edit** menu or key **F12** for DOS and use the cursor to highlight.
2. Select **Appearance** from the **Font** menu, followed by the enhancement you want. In the case of **Bold** and **Underline**, you can use function keys **F6** and **F8** instead.
3. The text is now shown in colour or highlighting on your screen, depending on your display. You can check enhancements when you preview.

Activity 3

1. Retrieve the text stored as **UNIT3-1**
2. Underline the headings as shown, using key **F8**
3. Save, preview and print one copy

WP OPERATORS

When operating a WP for any length of time it is important to ensure that working conditions are comfortable. If a few simple precautions are not observed, the work can lead to headaches and backaches.

DESK AND CHAIR

The workstation or desk should be at a comfortable height for the operator and an adjustable chair should be used so that the back is supported at all times whilst the feet are flat on the floor.

THE VDU

The VDU should be sited so that there is no reflection on the screen, which could cause eyestrain.

BREAKS

Breaks are important and an operator would be well advised not to work more than 2 hours at a VDU without a break.

3.4 Enhancing text as you key in

1 At the beginning of the text to be enhanced, select **Appearance** from the **Font** menu and choose the enhancement. For **Bold** or **Underline** only, use **F6** and **F8**.

2 Continue keying in to the end of the enhanced text, then select the enhancement again in exactly the same way, to stop the effect.

3 Key in the rest of the text, choosing effects and ending them, as required.

Activity 4

1 Key in the text given below, using underlining, bold text and italics as shown
2 Centre each line as shown and save as **UNIT3-2**
3 Proofread on screen and make any necessary changes
4 Print one copy

> **SAMSON COLLEGE OF ADULT EDUCATION**
>
> PHOTOGRAPHIC EXHIBITION
>
> *10 March 9 am - 5 pm*
>
> **Admission Free**

Activity 5

1 Key in the text given below, using underlining and bold text as shown
2 Centre the headings as shown
3 Check the display and make any necessary corrections
4 Save the text as **UNIT3-3** and print one copy

> **WESTERHAM HOTEL**
>
> **ANTIQUES VALUATION EVENING**
>
> 7 July 7.30 pm - 10 pm
>
> **Featuring Arthur Nolty (from Southalls)**
>
> Bring your treasures for valuation
>
> Tickets £10 including a glass of wine and buffet
>
> All enquiries to Kate Fairmont (0509 884521)
> Westerham Hotel, Courts, Leics LE1 5PQ

Further uses

1 Emphasising the subject in a letter

2 Emphasising the subject of a memo or report

3 Empasising side headings

4 Highlighting important issues in a document

Problem solving

- *Some of the text on a line which you centred is at the beginning of the line.*

  The cursor was not at the beginning of the line when you selected the command to centre. Move the cursor to the beginning of the centred text and press Backspace delete to remove the centring code. Then move the cursor to the beginning of the line and centre again.

- *One or more of the characters, probably the last one, is not highlighted as you intended.*

  You did not select all the characters before highlighting. Perhaps your cursor or mouse pointer was *on* the last character, rather than *after* it? Select the character(s) a second time and highlight again.

- *Text following the piece you intended to underline is also underlined.*

  You did not select underlining again at the end of the text to switch off the enhancement. Position the cursor on the first character of the underlining and press Backspace delete to remove the underlining code. Then follow the procedure to underline existing text.

- *Text following the piece you intended to embolden is also bold.*

  You did not select emboldening again at the end of the text to switch off the enhancement. Position the cursor on the first character of the bold text and press Backspace delete to remove the emboldening code. Then follow the procedure to embolden existing text.

- *You cannot tell on a monchrome screen whether text is underlined or not.*

  You have not followed all the instructions given in **Preparing to use Wordperfect**. The default colour set for underlining is unsuitable for monochrome screens. Select **Setup** from the **File** menu, followed by **Display** and **Colour/Fonts/Attributes**. You can then select **Screen Colours**. Choosing colours **B** for Foreground and **H** for Background will give a reasonable level of contrast.

Unit 4

Notices and programmes

Overview Notices and programmes can be made attractive using simple display features such as vertical and horizontal centring, underlining, emboldening, changes in text size, italics and right alignment.

Existing skills

- Entering and editing text, saving and retrieving files - Units 1 and 2
- Centring a single line of text - Unit 3
- Enhancing text and using blocks - Units 2 and 3

New skills

- Centring a block of text
- Centring text vertically on a page
- Previewing text to check display
- Aligning text to the right margin
- Changing text size

Important Vertical centring is not shown on screen, except when previewing. So long as the paper in the printer is correctly set it will, however, be correct when printing.

MENU

Fresh Asparagus
Country Paté

Chicken Marengo
Vegetarian Lasagne

Strawberries and cream
Raspberry Bombe

Cheese and biscuits

Coffee with mints

4.1 Vertical centring

Notices look best if they are in the middle of the page. Using Word Perfect, horizontal centring is shown on screen, but vertical centring only in preview.

1 Move your cursor to the beginning of the first line of your text and select **Page** from the **Layout** menu.

2 Select **Centre Page** followed by **Y**es to set vertical centring.

3 Press **F7** to return to your text and **Save** it to disk.

Activity 1

1 If you have already completed Unit 3, so **UNIT3-3** is saved to disk, retrieve it and display it on screen
or
If the file is not on disk, key in the text given below, using the display shown. Use underlining, bold and italics as shown
2 Centre lines of text horizontally, as shown
3 Centre the text vertically on the page
4 Save the text with filename **UNIT4-1**

WESTERHAM HOTEL

ANTIQUES VALUATION EVENING

7 July 7.30 pm - 10 pm

Featuring Arthur Nolty (from Southalls)

Bring your treasures for valuation

Tickets £10 including a glass of wine and buffet

All enquiries to Kate Fairmont (0509 884521)
Westerham Hotel, Courts, Leics LE1 5PQ

Activity 2

1 If you have completed Unit 3 and so **UNIT3-2** is saved to disk, retrieve it
or
If the file is not on disk, key in the text given below, following the display as shown
2 Centre the text vertically
3 Save the text with filename **UNIT4-2**

> **SAMSON COLLEGE OF ADULT EDUCATION**
>
> PHOTOGRAPHIC EXHIBITION
>
> *10 March 9 am - 5 pm*
>
> **Admission Free**

4.2 Previewing text

Previewing text before you print it allows you to check the display before printing. You can see the whole page, or part of the page, exactly as it should come out on the printer you are using, with the correct type styles and sizes.

1 Display your text on screen, retrieving it from disk if necessary.

2 Select **Print** from the **File** menu, followed by **View Document** to see your text on screen.

3 Press **1**, **2** or **3** to view your text at the 3 possible scales.

4 Press **F7** to return to your text.

Activity 3

1 Retrieve the file **UNIT4-1**, if it is not already on screen
2 Preview the text to check the display
3 Make any necessary changes to the display and print out a copy

Activity 4

1 Retrieve the file **UNIT4-2**, if it is not already on screen
2 Preview the text to check the display
3 Make any necessary changes to the display and print out a copy

4.3 Centring an existing block of text

It is not necessary to centre each line of text individually, although this is the easiest way to work if only headings are being centred. Instead you can centre a number of lines at once, or even a complete page of text. This will work as long as there are no intermediate lines which are not to be centred.

1 Move the cursor to the beginning of the first line in the set of lines to be centred.

2 Select **Justify** from the **Layout** menu, followed by **Centre**.

3 Move the cursor to the beginning of the line after the lines being centred.

4 Select **Justify** from the **Layout** menu.

5 Select **Left**.

Important Justification is an example of a feature which is used continuously until it is superseded by a new setting.

Activity 5

1 Retrieve the text stored as **UNIT4-1**

2 Centre the whole notice as shown

3 Save, preview and print one copy

WESTERHAM HOTEL

ANTIQUES VALUATION EVENING

7 July 7.30 pm - 10 pm

Featuring Arthur Nolty (from Southalls)

Bring your treasures for valuation

Tickets £10 including a glass of wine and buffet

All enquiries to Kate Fairmont (0509 884521) Westerham Hotel, Courts, Leics LE1 5PQ

4.4 Centring all text while keying in

1 Clear the screen to key in a new file.

2 Before entering any text, select **Justify** from the **Layout** menu.

3 Select **Centre**.

4 Key in the text as normal. It will be centred automatically, as this format has been selected.

5 When ordinary left justified text is required again, select **Justify** from the **Layout** menu. Select **Left** and continue keying in.

Activity 6

1 Key in the text below, using **Layout Justify** to begin and end centring
2 Apply underline and bold as shown
3 Preview and make any necessary changes
4 Save as file **UNIT4-3** and print one copy

SAMSON COLLEGE OF ADULT EDUCATION

A MUSICAL EVENING WITH KENNETH HAYNES

30 April at 8 pm

Spring is here
Lilacs
Chrysanthemums
In Nature's Realm
Flower Song

4.5 Text alignment

As well as justifying a line or lines, individual words and phrases can be left, centre and right aligned on the same line.

Main part of ticket

Price		**Concessions**
£5.50	*Includes wine or orange juice*	£4.50

4.6 Aligning text to the right margin

Programmes for concerts, plays and other artistic events are often designed with the names of the artistes, composers, etc, lined up at the right margin in the same line as the name of the item. This feature is also useful for footers and headers, where left justified, centred and right aligned text may all be required in the same line.

You can right align existing text or you can align as you key in.

1. With the cursor immediately before the text to be right aligned, select **Align** from the **Layout** menu, followed by **Flush Right**.
2. Key in the text to be aligned, if necessary.
3. Press **Return** at the end of the line to end right alignment.

Activity 7

1. Retrieve the part programme saved as **UNIT4-3**
2. Key in the remaining items and composers, using Right Align to line up the composers' names
3. Vertically centre the text
4. Preview to check the display and make any necessary corrections
5. Print out one copy

SAMSON COLLEGE OF ADULT EDUCATION

A MUSICAL EVENING WITH KENNETH HAYNES

30 April at 8 pm

Spring is here	Rodgers
Lilacs	Rachmaninov
Chrysanthemums	Puccini
In Nature's Realm	Dvorak
Flower Song	Gounod
Country Gardens	Grainger
Green Tulips	Mayerl
A Rose Blooming	Brahms
Nights in the Gardens of Spain	Falla
Forest Murmurs	Wagner

4.7 Changing text size

The text sizes you can use depend on the printer you are using. WordPerfect provides 5 possible sizes apart from normal from which to choose: Fine, Small, Large, Very Large and Extra Large. To find out how these sizes look, print out the file **PRINTER.TST**, which should be on your disk as part of the set up procedure.

1 Mark the word or block of text which is to have its size changed, using the mouse or by selecting **Block** from the **Edit** menu (*see* Unit 2).

2 Select the **Font** menu and then the size you want from the list displayed.

3 Preview to make sure that your selection is correct.

Important If you choose Very Large or Extra Large text for a heading, you will probably need 2 blank lines after it, otherwise it will look very cramped.

Activity 8

1 Clear the screen, if necessary
2 Key in the text for the ticket shown below, leaving 2 blank lines after each of the large headings
3 Use right alignment and centring to produce the display given
4 Preview to check the display and text sizes
5 Make any changes necessary, save as **UNIT4-4** and print a copy

ST PETER'S SOCIAL CLUB

Present:

Old Tyme Music Hall

8 pm Saturday 2 March

at the Church Hall

Tickets £2.50

Senior Citizens **£2**
Children under 12 **£1.25**

Further uses

1 Producing tickets for fetes, concerts, parties

2 Producing invitations for parties, weddings and other celebrations

3 Making simple handbills and advertisements

4 Once you have learned how to change paper size for labels (*see* Unit 16), you will be able to use these facilities to make smaller tickets and labels, fitting as many as 6 on an A4 sheet for printing

Problem solving

- *Your vertically centred text is not in the middle of the page. It is nearer to the top of the page.*

  You have some extra unwanted blank lines *below* your text, which have been used in WordPerfect's centring calculations. Delete them by positioning the cursor at the beginning of each blank line in turn and pressing the Delete key.

- *Your vertically centred text is nearer to the bottom of the page than the top.*

  You have some extra unwanted lines *above* your text, which have been used in WordPerfect's centring calculations. Delete them as above.

- *One or more items in the concert programme is not aligned to the right margin.*

  You missed out the code for Right Alignment in one or more lines. Move the cursor to the first character of the item to be aligned and insert the code, using **Align** from **Layout** menu, followed by **Flush Right**.

- *One or more of the characters you enlarged, probably the last one, is not the same size as the others.*

  You did not select all the characters before enlarging. Perhaps your cursor or mouse pointer was on the last character, rather than after it? Select the character(s) a second time and choose the size again.

- *Your lines of enlarged text are very cramped when printed, perhaps even overlapping.*

  You did not leave 2 blank lines between them. Position the cursor in the blank line between the lines of text and press **Return** to insert an additional line.

Unit 5

Indented paragraphs

Overview A paragraph may be indented from both margins to give emphasis. To give a neat appearance to numbered paragraphs, the text can be indented to the first tab position, leaving the numbers clearly displayed at the left margin.

Existing skills

- Deleting text - Unit 2
- Inserting text - Unit 2
- Retrieving a file from disk - Unit 2

New skills

- Setting a temporary left margin
- Indenting paragraphs
- Revealing codes

Important Any problems with display can often be easily identified and solved by revealing the codes which you have inserted into your text. You can then delete the existing codes and insert corrected ones.

```
This paragraph is not indented at all, but goes from one
margin to the other.↵
↵
1  This is a numbered, indented paragraph, where the text
   is set to a temporary left margin, until you press
   Return at the end of the paragraph.↵
↵
   This is a fully indented paragraph, where the whole
   paragraph is inset from the left and right margin.
   This feature also lasts until the Return key is
   pressed at the end of the paragraph.↵
```

5.1 Numbering and indenting existing text

When numbered points are used, as in this text, the most attractive display is to indent the whole paragraph after the number. This gives a temporary left margin.

1 Position the cursor at the beginning of the first paragraph which is to have a number inserted and key in the number.

2 Select **Align** from the **Layout** menu, followed by **Indent ->**.

3 The text in the paragraph will move to begin at the first tab setting.

Activity 1

1 If you have already completed Unit 3 and so have **UNIT3-1** saved to disk, retrieve it, delete all headings except the first one and the extra blank lines
or
If this file is not on disk, key in the text given below, leaving one clear line between each paragraph

2 Save the text as **UNIT3-1**

```
                    WP OPERATORS

When operating a WP for any length of time it is important
to ensure that working conditions are comfortable.  If a
few simple precautions are not observed, the work can lead
to headaches and backaches.

The workstation or desk should be at a comfortable height
for the operator and an adjustable chair should be used so
that the back is supported at all times whilst the feet
are flat on the floor.

The VDU should be sited so that there is no reflection on
the screen, which could cause eyestrain.

Breaks are important and an operator would be well advised
not to work more than 2 hours at a VDU without a break.
```

Activity 2

1 Retrieve the file **UNIT3-1**, if it is not already on screen
2 Put in numbers and indents as shown below
3 Check the display through preview
4 Check the spelling
5 Save and print one copy

```
                         WP OPERATORS

1 When operating a WP for any length of time it is
  important to ensure that working conditions are
  comfortable.  If a few simple precautions are not
  observed, the work can lead to headaches and backaches.

2 The workstation or desk should be at a comfortable
  height for the operator and an adjustable chair should
  be used so that the back is supported at all times
  whilst the feet are flat on the floor.

3 The VDU should be sited so that there is no reflection
  on the screen, which could cause eyestrain.

4 Breaks are important and an operator would be well
  advised not to work more than 2 hours at a VDU without a
  break.
```

5.2 Numbering and indenting new text

1 Key in any titles and headings.

2 When you come to the beginning of the paragraph to be indented, type the number.

3 Immediately, select **Align** from the **Layout** menu, followed by **Indent->**.

4 Type the paragraph. The text will begin at the indented temporary margin until you press **Return** at the end of the paragraph.

5 Press **Return** again for a blank line, then repeat the process.

Activity 3

1 Clear the screen, if necessary
2 Key in the text shown below, numbering and indenting as you go
3 Proofread and make any amendments, save as **UNIT5-1** and print one copy

> **Advantages of Word Processing**
>
> 1 Reduces repetitive typing. Standard documents can be reproduced automatically and individual details added.
>
> 2 Enables redrafts to be made easily; insertions, deletions and block moves save retyping.
>
> 3 Facilitates the production of immaculate work.

5.3 Insetting paragraphs

With the cursor at the beginning of the paragraph to be inset, select **Align** from the **Layout** menu, followed by **Indent-><-**.

Activity 4

1 If you have completed Unit 2 and have the amended version of **UNIT1-1** on disk, retrieve it
or
Key in the text below beginning each paragraph at the left margin
2 Inset the second paragraph at both sides, as shown. Save and print

> Word processing has steadily increased in popularity since the early 1970s. Operators have been delighted with the ease of keyboarding and the facilities for correction and editing. Repetitive typing has become a thing of the past and all work can be produced to a very high standard.
>
> > Even if you are not familiar with the keyboard, you can still use a word processor to good advantage because of the ease of correction. Many operators use a spelling check program to aid in proofreading their work. Although a checker will not pick up such mistakes as 'know' for 'now', it will identify many mistypes.
>
> Word processing is very popular with home users and the cost of the machines has dropped so dramatically during recent years, that they have become within the reach of many users who had previously been content with a manual, electric or electronic typewriter.

5.4 Revealing codes

Invisible codes are inserted into your text to set display and printing features. They can be displayed on a secondary screen if you want to examine them or delete them.

1 With your text displayed on screen, press key **F11** or select **Reveal Codes** from the **Edit** menu.

2 The screen will be split near the bottom, and a second version of your text will be shown, with codes displayed in square brackets.

3 As you move your cursor, a cursor will move with it in the secondary screen, highlighting codes as it moves over them.

5.5 Removing indentation

1 With your text displayed on screen, reveal codes.

2 Move the cursor to the indented paragraph.

3 Position the cursor to highlight the code **[Indent->]** or **[Indent-><-]** and use the Delete key to remove it. The text will move back to the margin.

Activity 5

1 Retrieve the file **UNIT3-3**
2 Delete the numbers and temporary indents and inset the third paragraph 3, as shown
3 Save and print one copy

```
                     WP OPERATORS

When operating a WP for any length of time it is important
to ensure that working conditions are comfortable.  If a
few simple precautions are not observed, the work can lead
to headaches and backaches.

The workstation or desk should be at a comfortable height
for the operator and an adjustable chair should be used so
that the back is supported at all times whilst the feet
are flat on the floor.

    The VDU should be sited so that there is no ref-
    lection on the screen, which could cause eyestrain.

Breaks are important and an operator would be well advised
not to work more than 2 hours at a VDU without a break.
```

Further uses

1 Indented paragraphs save leaving an extra line space between paragraphs when working in double line spacing

2 Inset paragraphs can be used to highlight prices or other important items in a letter

Problem solving

- *There is no gap between the number and the first character of the top line of text in your numbered pararaphs.*

  You did not select the Indent code immediately after keying in the number. Reveal codes to display and delete the Indent code. Then move the cursor immediately after the number and follow the instructions to number and indent existing text.

- *You cannot move your cursor to the code you want to delete in the secondary window.*

  You can only move the cursor with the left and right cursor key in this window at the very beginning of the file, where there are a number of codes. Use left and right cursor to highlight the code.

- *Your inset paragraph in Activity 5 is too far from the left margin.*

  You did not delete the indent code before you inset the paragraph, so it is doubly indented. Reveal codes, if necessary, and delete the **[Indent->]** code.

Unit 6

Business letters

Overview The display used in most business letters is very similar. With word processing, you can use a letter you have sent before as the basis for a new one. You can also compose a standard or basic letter from a library of macros (standard words or phrases). Updating can also be achieved with search and replace.

Existing skills

- Emboldening text - Unit 3
- Numbered paragraphs - Unit 5

New skills

- Inserting standard text using a macro
- Inserting the date automatically
- Replacing words and phrases automatically
- Replacing words and phrases selectively

Important The sample given on the right is the standard layout used in most business letters. It may vary a little, according to a house style in a particular organisation, but this display will always be acceptable. In any case, all the items listed will be needed.

Heading with firm's name

Our Ref:

Today's date

Name
Address

Dear ????

Subject heading

Substance of letter

Yours sincerely

Name of person signing letter
Title of job

6.1 Entering a letter

1 Key in your text using blocked display, ie all lines begin at the left margin, with no indentation, and open puncuation, ie punctuation only in the sentences in the main body of the letter.

2 To insert today's date, select **Date code** from the **Tools** menu.

3 Proofread and preview, before saving and printing.

Activity 1

1 Key in the letter shown below, starting all lines at the left margin
2 Embolden the subject heading
3 Spell check to check your text for typing mistakes, then make any necessary corrections
4 Save as **UNIT6-1**, preview and print

Today's date

Mr M Shah
311 Gelford Road
LEICESTER
LE10 5GR

Dear Mr Shah

Wednesday Club Supper, 5 May

With reference to our telephone conversation of yesterday, I write to confirm that I would be happy to prepare a cold buffet for your group at a cost of £3 per head.

However, as I explained to you on the telephone, should you want a hot meal, the cheapest I could provide would be £3.95 for either plaice or egg and chips, served with a selection of vegetables and a salad garnish.

I look forward to receiving your confirmation of final numbers and menu choice in the near future. If I can be of any further assistance, please do give me a ring.

Yours sincerely

Kerry Asher

Enc

6.2 Setting up a phrase as a stored macro

1 Select **Macro** from the **Tools** menu, followed by **Define**.

2 Key in a name for your macro of 8 or less characters, preferably one you will remember easily, and press **Return**.

3 Press **Return** again to bypass the *Description:* message.

4 Type the phrase, exactly as you want it to be stored. For example, it may need an accompanying extra blank line, so 2 Returns are needed after it.

5 Select **Macro** from the **Tools** menu, followed by **Define** again to end the macro definition.

6 Press **Return** to go to a new line and set up the next macro in the same way.

6.3 Using a macro to insert a stored phrase

1 Position the cursor in the text where the phrase is to be inserted.

2 Select **Macro** from the **Tools** menu, followed by **Execute**.

3 At the message, enter the name of your stored macro and press **Return**.

Activity 2

1 Clear the screen, if necessary
2 Set up the 10 phrases given in the table below as macros, using the names suggested. The symbol ↵ after the text means press **Return** for an additional blank line
3 Execute all of the macros to make sure they work, proofread and spell check
4 Replace any macros which need corrections by setting them up again with the same name and selecting **Replace**

PHRASE	SUGGESTED FILE NAME
Dear Sir ↵	SIR
Dear Madam ↵	MADAM
Thank you for your letter.	THANK
With reference to our telephone conversation	PHONE
I shall look forward to hearing from you. ↵	HEAR
With best wishes ↵	WISHES
Yours faithfully ↵ ↵ ↵ ↵	YRFAITH
Yours sincerely ↵ ↵ ↵ ↵	YRSINC
Douglas Osiejuk ↵	DO
Enc	E

6.4 Using macros in a letter

1 Key in the letter as normal, starting all lines at the left margin.

2 At points where an appropriate macro has been stored, select **Macro Execute** from the **Tools** menu to insert the stored phrase.

Activity 3

1 Key in the letter given below, using macros to insert stored phrases. The ones which are available are marked with a box

2 Check that you have the correct spacing, insert any additional blank lines which you require, save as **UNIT6-2** and print

```
Today's date

Clerk to Northwood Parish Council
29 Windmill Lane
Northwood
North Devon
EX39 2JB

[Dear Sir]

Maintenance of Northwood Playing Field

[With reference to our telephone conversation] of today, I
have pleasure in submitting the following quotation for the
maintenance of Northwood Playing Field:

21 cuts to Cricket Square and Cricket Pitch.

9 mows/strims of field surrounds, including play area,
surrounding pavilion and in front of tennis courts and
around the saplings alongside the field.

All areas to be maintained using own equipment and fuel.

Price £1100

[I shall look forward to hearing from you.]

[Yours sincerely]



[Douglas Osiejuk]
```

6.5 Selective search and replace

1 Select **Replace** from the **Search** menu and at the message *w/Confirm?* ***No*** *(Yes)* select **Yes** to allow you to choose whether any instance is to be replaced.

2 At the message *->Srch,* key in the exact characters to be replaced followed by key **F7**.

3 At the message *Replace with*, key in the replacement phrase and key **F7**.

4 As each occurrence is highlighted, select **Yes** or **No** to choose.

Activity 4

1 Key in the letter given below, using standard letter layout and inserting the current date automatically
2 Use selective replacement to change the colour of the clothes from Black to Grey
3 Save as **UNIT6-3** and print one copy

```
Today's date

Ms A Black
Manageress
E & G Modes
Avebury Way
MILTON KEYNES   MK14 ORD

Dear Ms Black

Thank you for your telephone enquiry today regarding our
summer range of 'Ginelli'.  I have in stock the following
fashions which I think will fulfil your requirements:

5 Rose pink suits, sizes 12-14 @ £200 each
10 Black and white two pieces, sizes 10-16 @ £150 each
20 Black spot skirts, sizes 10-16 @ £70 each
20 Black spot blouses, sizes 10-16 @ £59 each
8 Black summer jackets @ £79 each

I look forward to hearing from you.

Yours sincerely



Nicholos Selepegno
Managing Director
```

6.6 Automatic search and replace

1 Select **Replace** from the **Search** menu and at the message *w/Confirm?* ***No*** *(Yes)* select **No** to allow replacement automatically.

2 Follow the same process as for selective search and replace (6.5).

3 All occurrences of the phrase will be replaced.

Activity 5

1 Key in the letter given below, using standard letter layout and inserting the current date automatically
2 Use automatic replacement to change the price quoted from £90 to £150
3 Save as **UNIT6-4** and print one copy

Today's date

Mr & Mrs C Bates
6 Milwood Road
GILLINGHAM
KENT
ME7 5LN

Dear Mr & Mrs Bates

Thank you for your enquiry.

I have a special offer on 3-day breaks at the moment at £90 per person. This includes a double room with bath, breakfast and evening meal.

I can also offer you deluxe accommodation on 2-day breaks, half board, at the special price of £90 per person. In addition to a double room with bath, a sitting room is included.

These advantageous offers at £90 per person are for a limited time only and are proving very popular.

I shall look forward to hearing from you.

Yours sincerely

Paul Colicos
Manager

Many organisations send out letters which are repetitive and set up WP libraries with standard paragraphs.

Activity 6

1 The following are a selection of paragraphs from the WP library of a bank, set up to enable the automatic composition of repetitive letters
2 Set up each paragraph as a macro, without a number, naming them **PARA1**, **PARA2**, etc
3 Insert each macro in turn on to the screen, so that you have a complete list of them. Number them as shown and print out for reference
4 Compose a letter to Mrs N Turner, 36 The Willows, High Wycombe, Bucks HP13 7TB, using today's date and paragraphs 4 and 10. Print one copy
5 Compose a letter to Mr A Watts, 115 Green Street, High Wycombe, Bucks HP10 3HW, using today's date and paragraphs 6 and 9. Print one copy

1 I have noticed that your account is slightly overdrawn and, although cheques are still being processed, this situation cannot be allowed to continue.

2 I regret that your account is very much overdrawn and, in these circumstances, no more cheques can be honoured.

3 I regret that you have suffered some embarrassment because your cheques could not be honoured. Your account is very much overdrawn and this matter was called to your attention. I am afraid that, unless there is a considerable cash injection to the account, cheques cannot be processed.

4 I regret that you were charged for safe custody in your last statement although you have no documents in our custody. The charges will be reimbursed in your next statement.

5 It has come to my attention that you are maintaining quite a large balance in your current account. I think it would be to your advantage to change over to an interest cheque account.

6 There have been one or two problems with your account. It would be advantageous if we met to discuss the situation.

7 I wonder if you are aware that we offer a financial advice service. If you are interested in investing your money for the very best return, please make an appointment to see our financial advisor, Mr S Walters. He will be pleased to assist you and, of course, there is no obligation to take his advice.

8 I regret that you have not been satisfied with our service and I think that a full discussion would be of benefit.

9 I should be grateful if you would make an appointment to see me. Please ring my secretary for a mutually convenient date.

10 I regret any inconvenience which has been caused and can assure you that this mistake will not happen again.

Further uses

1 Storing standard paragraphs for legal documents

2 Storing words and phrases you use frequently, or have difficulty in remembering

3 Saving typing

Problem solving

- *All occurrences of a word have been changed, instead of only some which you wanted to choose.*

  When you selected **Replace**, you pressed Return at the message *w/confirm? No (Yes)* instead of selecting **Yes**. Select **Replace** again, and replace the new word with the old one. Then selectively replace the words again.

- *The £ symbol is not displayed on screen or in preview.*

  You need to change your keyboard setting. In many cases, the selection of £ happens automatically, but if £ is not displayed, follow this procedure.

  Select **Setup** from the **File** menu, followed by **Keyboard Layout** and **Map**. A diagram of keyboard assignments will be displayed on screen. Move the cursor to the **#** symbol on the third set of keys. Select **Compose** and key in **4,11** and **Return**, to enter the keyboard setting and number of the £ symbol in WordPerfect. Press **F7** to return to your text and try the £ key. It should now give a £ on screen.

- *You have numbers for the paragraphs in your letter in Activity 6.*

  You keyed the numbers, as well as the paragraphs to be saved, and highlighted them for the macros. You will have to set up your macros again, without the numbers, to use them in the future. To correct your letter, just delete the numbers from it, and reveal codes to make sure there are no unwanted indentation codes.

Unit 7

Personal letters

Overview Personal letters use a similar format to business letters, but with the addition of the writer's home address on the right hand side at the top. There is a good deal of standard information which can be set up to use as a template for all future letters.

Existing skills

- Enhancing text - Unit 3
- Revealing codes - Unit 5
- Generating the date automatically - Unit 6

New skills

- Setting tabs
- Setting up a template
- Displaying the tab ruler
- Saving a file with a new name

Important When setting tabs, it is a good idea to Reveal Codes, so that you can see the Tab command on screen, as shown below.

```
This is the beginning of the file.



C:\WP51\JUNK
[   ▲    ▲    ▲    ▲    ▲    ▲    ▲    ▲    ▲    ▲    ▲
[Tab Set: Abs: 0", every 0.5"]This is the beginning of the
file.[HRt]


Press Reveal Codes to restore screen
```

7.1 Displaying the current tabs and margins

The tabs and margins ruler is not normally displayed on screen, but it is useful to be able to see it, if you are going to make any changes.

1 Select **Window** from the **Edit** menu.

2 The message *Number of lines in this window: 22* will be displayed at the foot of the screen. Key in **21** and press Return.

3 The editing screen will be reduced to 21 lines and the bottom line will be used to display the ruler across the screen.

7.2 Setting tabs

By default, tabs are set at 1/2" intervals. For many purposes, this will be acceptable, but sometimes you want different or fewer tabs.

1 With the cursor at the beginning of the file, select **Line** from the **Layout** menu, followed by **8** or Tab Set.

2 Move the cursor to the extreme left of the ruler line displayed, and select **Delete EOL** (End Of Line) to clear all the pre-set tabs.

3 Move the cursor to each point where a tab is required and press **L**.

4 Press **F7** or the right mouse button twice to confirm and return to the text.

7.3 Setting up a format for personal letters

1 Set up a tab at about 5" from the left margin ie 1.5" from the right margin, to use for the address. Set the font to Oblique (Italic) style.

2 Type in your home address, remembering to press the Tab key for each line, so that the address is at the right hand side.

3 Insert the date automatically.

Activity 1

1 Clear the screen, if necessary, and then Reveal Codes
2 Display the ruler, set a tab at 5", delete the code which set the original tabs and set oblique font
3 Complete the format as shown below and save as **UNIT7-1**

```
                                        55 Garfield Street
                                        Teddington
                                        Middlesex
                                        TW11 9PX

Today's date
```

7.4 Saving a file with a new name

1 Load up an existing file.

2 Edit the text as required and then select **Save** from the **File** menu.

3 At the message *Document to be saved: <old file name>*, key your new file name and press Return. The file will be saved with the new name.

7.5 Using the personal letter format

1 Load up the file which holds the letter format.

2 Complete the letter and save with a new name, so that the letter format is still saved on disk.

3 Make any necessary corrections, save again and print.

Activity 2

1 Load up the personal letter format stored as **UNIT7-1**
2 Change the address given to your own, to make a template for your own letters
3 If you have a longer line in your address than those used in the example, then use Reveal Codes to delete the tab setting, and set one nearer to the left margin to accommodate this line. Alternatively, you may want to make the tab setting nearer the right margin, if you have very short lines
4 Save as **PERS-LET** and print one copy for reference

Activity 3

1 Load up the personal letter format stored as **UNIT7-1**
2 Complete the letter shown below, making sure that all the text is in italic style
3 Save as **UNIT7-2** and print one copy

55 Garfield Street
Teddington
Middlesex
TW11 9PX

Today's date

Mr & Mrs T Meldrum
Hollytree Cottage
Torrington
North Devon
EX11 5HT

Dear Babs and Tom

Thank you so much for a lovely week-end. I thoroughly enjoyed the fresh country air and the food was delicious, as always.

I had a good journey back and found the cat in good shape, thanks to my neighbour.

I shall look forward to seeing you next month at the Townsends'.

With best wishes

Problem solving

- *The address is not lined up correctly.*

  You did not press the Tab key at the beginning of each line. Reveal codes, if you have not already done so, and check that there is one **[Tab]** code on each line. Delete any extra ones, or insert any which are missing.

- *You have to press the Tab key more than once to move to the position for the address.*

  You have not set up the new tab setting correctly. Reveal codes, if you have not already done so, delete the faulty tab setting code and go through the process again.

Unit 8

Simple tables

Overview Most column work can be displayed by setting up tabs as part of the page layout, but a more powerful and flexible method is to use tables. Using these, you will be able to change the column settings easily.

Existing skills

- Centring text on entry - Unit 3
- Emboldening text - Unit 3

New skills

- Setting up a table
- Editing a table
- Totalling values in a table

Important Tables should be used in preference to tabs, as they are much more powerful, and considerably easier to change to accommodate amendments and insertions. They can also have their shape altered to fit the space available.

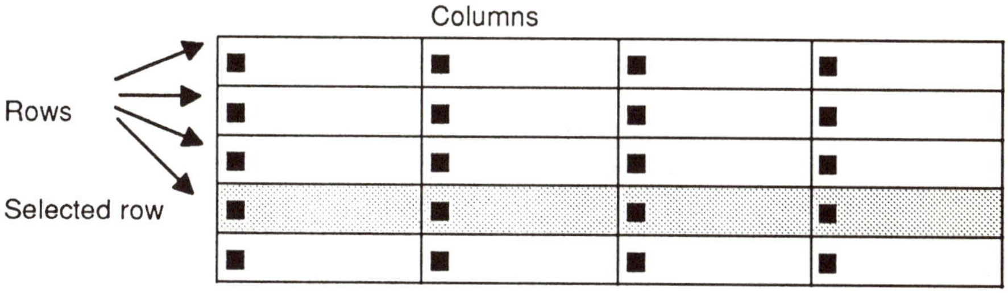

■	■	■	■
■	■	■	■
■	■	■	■
■	■	■	■
■	■	■	■

8.1 Creating a table

A table is specified by the number of columns and rows it has. When you define a new one, the number of columns you specify will set the column width, as the whole table will fill the space between margins.

1 Move your cursor to the position in the text where your table is to begin.

2 Select **Tables** from the **Layout** menu followed by **Create**.

3 At the message *Number of Columns: key in the number of columns you require and press* ***Return***.

4 At the message *Number of Rows: key in the number of rows you require and press* ***Return***.

5 A grid with the specified number of columns and rows will be displayed on screen, fitting the current margins. Each cell has gridlines and an insertion point displayed.

6 The **Table Edit** menu will be displayed at the foot of the screen, ready for you to make adjustments.

7 Press key **F7** or the right mouse button to Exit from the menu. Your cursor will be in the first cell ready for entry.

8 Use the cursor or mouse to select each cell and type in its contents.

Important You cannot enter contents into cells when the **Table Edit** menu is displayed.

Activity 1

1 If necessary, clear the screen and type in the title *A Demonstration Table* on the first line
2 With the cursor on the next line, create a table with 7 rows and 4 columns
3 Enter the information given below in the table cells as shown. You will notice that some cells will increase in height to fit the text
4 Preview to check the display
5 Save the title and table as **UNIT8-1**

VILLAGE HALL	SCHEME	COST	RECOMMENDATIO NS
■	■	£	£
Briarwood	New heating system	■	■
■	New kitchen units	6,500	3,250
Basilford	Replace flat roof	■	■
■	Replace ceiling	9,420	5,537
Deshall	Purchase of land	9,500	2,600

8.2 Changing column width

1 Position the cursor anywhere in the table and select **Table** from the **Layout** menu, followed by **Edit** and pressing the Esc key to display the **Table Edit** menu at the foot of the screen.

```
Table Edit:  Press Exit when finished   Cell A1 Doc 1 Pg 2 Ln 1.47" Pos 1.12"
================================================================================
Ctrl-Arrows Column Widths; Ins Insert; Del Delete; Move Move/Copy;
1 Size; 2 Format; 3 Lines; 4 Header; 5 Maths; 6 Options; 7 Join; 8 Split: 0
```

2 Move the cursor to each column whose width is to be adjusted, in turn.

3 Use the left and right cursor keys, while holding down the Ctrl key, to widen and narrow the selected column.

4 Press key **F7** or the left mouse button to Exit.

Important As the column width is set initially to fill the space between the margins, regardless of how many columns you want, you will have to narrow a column first, before there is space available to widen any other column.

8.3 Joining and splitting cells

If text is too wide to fit in one cell, as will often be the case with headings, you can combine adjacent cells to display the text, without having to change the width or height of a complete column or row. This is called joining. Splitting cells means making them into individual cells again.

1 Position the cursor in the first cell in the group to be joined.

2 Display the **Table Edit** menu, by selecting **Layout**, **Table**, **Edit** and pressing Esc, as before.

3 Press **Alt F4** to turn **Block on** and then move the cursor to highlight the other cells to be joined.

4 Select **7** or Join, and at the message *Join cells? No (Yes)*, select **Yes**.

5 The cells will be joined, and the line between them will disappear.

6 Type in the text right across the cells.

7 To split previously joined cells, highlight and select **8** or Split from the **Table Edit** menu.

Important Joining cells will not reformat text already in the cells. You must join cells first, then type in the long text.

Activity 2

1 Set up a table with 6 columns and 9 rows for the information given below
2 Join all the cells in the first row, before typing in the heading, centred and emboldened, as shown. *Use the normal methods for this, ie* ***Layout Align Centre*** *and* ***F6***
3 Key in the remaining cells, emboldening as shown
4 Narrow all columns except the second, then widen the second column, as shown below
5 Preview to check display, save as **UNIT8-2** and print

EXPENSES					
Month	**Details**	**Total**	**Miles**	**Misc**	**VAT**
March	150 miles @ 52.8p	79.20	79.20		
March	Photocopying	8.18		6.96	1.22
March	Printer ribbons	21.86		18.61	3.25
March	Parcel	0.28		0.28	
March	Taxi	10.00	10.00		
March	Trade booklet	0.50		0.50	

8.4 Inserting rows and columns

1 Move the cursor to the position where a row or column is to be inserted.

2 Display the **Table Edit** menu and press the **Insert** key.

3 At the message *Insert:* ***1*** *Rows;* ***2*** *Columns: 0* select Rows or Columns.

4 Key in the number of rows/columns to be inserted, then Return and Exit to the text.

Activity 3

1 Load up the file **UNIT8-1** which contains the table created in Activity 1
2 Insert a row for the heading, embolden and centre as shown
3 Adjust the column widths to fit the text, as shown
4 Preview, save with the same name and print

VILLAGE HALL GRANT APPLICATIONS			
VILLAGE HALL	**SCHEME**	**COST**	**RECOMMENDATIONS**
		£	**£**
Briarwood	New heating system		
	New kitchen units	6,500	3,250
Basilford	Replace flat roof		
	Replace ceiling	9,420	5,537
Deshall	Purchase of land	9,500	2,600

8.5 Adding a column of figures

Tables have calculations built in, such as adding columns of figures automatically, and more complicated formulae, for simple spreadsheet use.

1 Move the cursor to the cell where the total is to be displayed and display the **Table Edit** menu.

2 Select **5** or **M**aths followed by **2** or **F**ormula then key in **+**, the formula for column total, followed by **Return**.

3 The total of all the numbers in the column, ignoring all text, will be inserted into the cell.

4 Exit from the menu.

8.6 Copying a calculation

1 Select the cell containing the calculation and display the **Table Edit** menu.

2 Select **5** or **M**aths followed by **3** or Co**p**y Formula, then select **1** or **C**ell and move the cursor to the cell where the calculation is to go and press Return.

3 Exit from the menu.

Activity 4

1 Load up the file **UNIT8-2**, which contains a table
2 Insert an additional row at the top of the table for the main title, joining the cells before entering the title, centred and emboldened
3 Complete the bottom row with the title, total the third column automatically and then copy the calculation to the remaining columns
4 Preview the file to check display, save again and print

PRODUCTION DEPARTMENT					
EXPENSES					
Month	**Details**	**Total**	**Miles**	**Misc**	**VAT**
March	150 miles @ 52.8p	79.20	79.20		
March	Photocopying	8.18		6.96	1.22
March	Printer ribbons	21.86		18.61	3.25
March	Parcel	0.28		0.28	
March	Taxi	10.00	10.00		
March	Trade booklet	0.50		0.50	
	Total	120.02	89.20	26.35	4.47

Further uses

1 Quotations

2 Curriculum Vitae (*see* Unit 9)

3 Invoices (*see* Unit 11)

Problem solving

- *You cannot key information into your table, although it is displayed on screen.*

  The **Table Edit** menu is on screen. Press **F7** to Exit to your text.

- *You cannot widen a column to fit its contents.*

  You have not first narrowed a column, so your table fills the whole space between margins. Follow the procedure to narrow a column to make some space, and then try again.

- *You have joined two cells to accommodate a long piece of text, but the text in the first cell has not been reformatted to fit them.*

  You must key in the text **after** you join the cells, to make it fit the new cells. Delete the existing text and rekey it in the joined cell.

- *You cannot mark a block of cells to edit the lines or join the cells.*

  The usual menus cannot be used while the **Table Edit** menu is on screen. You have to use the function key method instead, ie press **Alt F4**, to go into block mode.

- *You have changed one of the figures in your table, but the column total is still the same as before.*

  Totals are not automatically recalculated when you change a value in a table. Display the **Table Edit** menu and select **Maths** followed by **Calculate**.

Unit 9

Itineraries and CVs

Overview

Some complicated tabulated work, which would be difficult using special tabs, can be accomplished with multi-line tables. This is particularly useful for displays which include side headings. It is always worth considering, when you are setting tabs, whether using a table would be more appropriate.

Existing skills

- Increasing the size of text - Unit 4
- Creating a table - Unit 8
- Editing a table - Unit 8

New skills

- Using lines in tables
- Using multi-line tables

The right line is wide for emphasis	Very long titles need several lines of text			

9.1 Removing lines from a table

When tables are used as an alternative to tabulation, no gridlines are required, as the text is intended to look like normal text.

1 Move the cursor to the top left cell and display the **Table Edit** menu.

2 Press **Alt F4** to turn Block on and move the cursor to highlight the complete table.

3 Select **3** or **L**ines followed by **7** or **A**ll and **1** or **N**one to remove all the lines. Exit from the menu.

9.2 Multi-line rows in a table

1 Key in the first line of the entry in a cell and press Return.

2 The row height will increase to fit in another line of text.

3 Key in the second and subsequent lines in the same cell.

Activity 1

1 Clear the screen, if necessary, and set up a table with 3 columns and 11 rows to contain the itinerary shown below, allowing a row for each item, however long, and one blank row between each item. *The row numbers are to show you where each entry is to go*

2 Remove all the lines, make any adjustments needed to column widths and embolden as shown

3 Save as **UNIT9-1** and print

1	**TRAVEL ITINERARY - Monday 6 April**		
2			
3	**Depart**	**Arrive**	**Details**
4			
5	0915	1100	London to Leicester
6			
7		1115	Patel's Wholesalers, 112 High Street Tel: 0509 780023
8			
9	1400	1530	Nottm - see Mr Simpson, 59 Market Street Tel: 0509 773421
10			
11	1730	1800	Grand Hotel, Shire Street Tel: 0509 708451

Activity 2

1 Set up a 2 column table to hold the CV given below, allowing one row for each item
2 Key in the side headings, then each entry, ending in an extra Return to give space between the items
3 Adjust the first column to fit the longest side heading
4 Save as **UNIT9-2** and print

CURRICULUM VITAE

NAME	Andrew Gere
ADDRESS	77 Thorn Road Bridlington N Humberside YO14 3BT
TELEPHONE	0262 632711
MARITAL STATUS	Single
NATIONALITY	British
EDUCATION	1983-85 King Edward School, Bradford 1985-87 Barside Technical College, Bradford
QUALIFICATIONS	GCSE in English, Geography, History, Mathematics and Music BTEC National Diploma in Business Studies
WORK EXPERIENCE	1987 to present Sales Executive with Barside Cars
HOBBIES/INTERESTS	Badminton, Football, Music
REFEREES	Mr N I Preedon, BSc, MEd, FRSA Principal Barside Technical College BRADFORD BD1 9RH Telephone: 0274 800432 Ms A Line Managing Director Barside Cars Cliff Road BRADFORD BD9 7CR Telephone: 0274 811045

Further uses

1 Any programme which can be split into columns, such as one for a concert or show

2 Handbills with side headings

3 Timetables

4 Weekly diaries

Problem solving

- *There are no gaps between a piece of text and the next side heading.*

  You have not typed a **Return** at the end of the text. Select the cell, move to the end of the text and press **Return**.

- *There are still some lines in your table.*

  You did not mark the whole table as a block before you formatted the lines. Move your cursor to the top left corner cell in the table, display the **Table Edit** menu and mark the block again.

- *Your line ends are not the same as in the samples.*

  Your table is considerably wider than the ones shown, as you are using A4 paper. Narrow the columns to reflect the display given.

Unit 10

Memos

Overview

An organisation will sometimes have special memo stationery, with a printed heading. Another option is to set up a standard heading using a template file. This can then be used whenever a memo is to be keyed in.

Existing skills

- Centring text - Unit 3
- Enhancing text - Unit 3
- Setting tabs - Unit 7
- Generating the date automatically - Unit 6

New skills

- Using End key to move cursor

Important Once you have set up a template, you should be careful not to alter the original version. You should *Write protect* it to be sure of this, ie either save it on a floppy disk which is then write protected or use the DOS command ATTRIB to protect it.

10.1 Setting up a memo template

1 Clear the screen, if necessary.

2 Clear the existing tabs and set tabs at .25" and 1.5".

3 Key in the main heading for your memo, using centred bold large text and double spaced letters.

4 Enter the standard side headings, separated by blank lines.

5 Check carefully, save and print.

Activity 1

1 Clear the screen, if necessary
2 Key in the following text to a new file, pressing the tab key after each side heading
3 Embolden and centre as shown
4 Save to disk as file **MEMO.TMP**

```
                    M E M O R A N D U M

Date:

To:

From:

Subject:
-----------------------------------------------------
```

10.2 Using the memo template

1 Load up the file which contains the memo template.

2 Save the file with a new name, so that the template is left unchanged.

3 Edit this file by adding the details for the particular memo you want to send, using the **End** key to move the cursor to the end of the line for each side heading.

4 Generate the date automatically.

5 Preview the file, to check the display.

6 Save and print.

Activity 2

1 Load up the file **MEMO.TMP**
2 Key in the memo given below
3 Save it as the file **UNIT10-1** and print

MEMORANDUM

Date: Today's date

To: All Staff

From: Manager

Subject: Stock Taking

Stock taking will take place next Sunday, commencing at 1630 hours. It is expected that all staff will take part. Normal Sunday overtime rates will apply or time off in lieu may be arranged with your Supervisor.

Activity 3

1 Load up the file **MEMO.TMP**
2 Key in the memo given below
3 Save it as the file **UNIT10-2** and print

MEMORANDUM

Date: Today's date

To: All Supervisors

From: Manager

Subject: Official Opening

There will be a meeting in my office next Monday morning at 8.30 am in connection with the official opening. Please arrange your duties so that you will be able to attend. The meeting should not take more that half an hour.

Further uses

1 Template files may be set up for any standard documents eg letters, reports, contracts

2 It is useful to create a template with a frequently used letter heading as in an organisation's details or a personal address

Problem solving

- *You have saved your corrected version of the memo with the same name as before, overwriting the original.*

  If you followed the instructions correctly in Preparing to Use WordPerfect, you will have a backup copy of the memo template, called MEMO.BK! on disk. You can rename it and then retrieve it and use it again.

- *Your screen and keyboard have jammed. You cannot enter any more text.*

  It is possible that you have typed a large number of hyphens for your ruling line on the memo very quickly, and more than filled the keyboard buffer. This buffer stores key presses until the machine has time to display them on screen. On a very few machine models, this will cause a catastropic failure. Press the Reset button, if you have one, or alternatively, hold down **Ctrl** and **Alt** and tap the **Delete** key to reset the machine. Load up WordPerfect again. Type the hyphens more slowly next time!

Unit 11

Invoices

Overview When you are producing invoices and other documents which involve numbers, you can use the mathematical features of WordPerfect tables to do the calculations. You might also find it useful to use any additional fonts your printer can produce to make an attractive heading.

Existing skills

- Changing text size - Unit 4
- Setting up and editing a table - Unit 8
- Totalling values in a table - Unit 8
- Using lines in tables - Unit 9

New skills

- Changing fonts
- Using formulae in tables

Important A font is a typeface, which can be produced in a number of point sizes [72 points = 1"] and a number of weights, i.e. bold, medium and light. A few examples are given below.

TYPE OF FONT	NAME	FEATURES
Sans Serif	Helvetica/Swiss	Plain characters with no extra strokes
Serif	Times Roman	Small characters with extra strokes
Monospaced	Courier	All characters are the same width
Script	*Chancery*	Handwritten joined letter style

11.1 Changing fonts

1. Before entering text, or after highlighting existing text, select **Base Font** from the **Font** menu.
2. From the list of fonts, sizes and styles, highlight the one you want.
3. Press **1** or **S**elect to select the highlighted font and continue keying in text until a different font is required.

Activity 1

1. Clear the screen and key in text in each font you have on your printer. Choose a sans serif font, if available, closest in appearance to the Helvetica used in the invoice heading
2. Clear the screen and choose A4 or 11" continuous paper
3. Key in the invoice heading given below, following the display and alignment, and using the sans serif you have chosen for the heading
4. Save as **INVOICE.TMP** to use as an invoice template, preview and print

I N V O I C E No **0000**

K B BROWN (CONTRACTORS) LTD

BUILDING AND CIVIL ENGINEERS
Station Close
Nottingham — Phone: 0602 894571
NG1 7CS — Fax: 0602 893156

Date:
Customer name

VAT NO: 233 4532 21

Activity 2

1. Load up **INVOICE.TMP** saved in Activity 1, insert a blank line before the VAT number and move the cursor there
2. Set up a 2 column, 3 row table for the values below. Enter the text and use **Table Maths** and the + function to give the final total
3. Delete all gridlines, then enter top and bottom lines for the bottom right cell, as shown.
4. Save as **UNIT11-1** and print one copy

To works completed in accordance with your letter dated 1 August	
VAT @ 17.5%	
TOTAL	

Activity 3

1 Load up **UNIT11-1**
2 Enter the details for the invoice shown below, including the price and VAT, following the display
3 Use **Maths Calculate** from the **Table Edit** menu to perform the calculation for the total price
4 Preview to check the display, save and print one copy

I N V O I C E No **7918**

K B BROWN (CONTRACTORS) LTD

BUILDING AND CIVIL ENGINEERS
Station Close
Nottingham
NG1 7CS

Telephone: 0602 894571
Fax: 0602 893156

10 October 19..

Mr L Tomlins
307 Upperton Road
NOTTINGHAM
NG10 9UR

New Retaining Wall, Hales Fields, Nottingham

To works completed in accordance with your letter dated 1 August	2,122.00
VAT @ 17.5%	371.35
TOTAL	2,493.35

VAT NO: 233 4532 21

11.2 Using formulae in tables

You have used already the special function + to add columns of figures, in Activity 3. As well as this sort of special function, you can use general formulae in tables, similar to those used in simple spreadsheets. You will find these listed in the manual.

The cells in a table are labelled in exactly the same way as spreadsheets for reference in formulae by column letter and row number, eg B3.

Column letters

		A	B	C	D
	1				
	2				
Row numbers	3		Cell B3		
	4				
	5				
	6				

1 Create the table, key in the text and figures and adjust the column widths to display the information sensibly.

2 Move the cursor to the cell in which the formula is to be entered, ie the one in which the *answer* to the calculation is to be displayed.

3 Display the **Table Edit** menu and select **Maths**, followed by **2** or **F**ormula.

4 Enter the formula, using cell references and arithmetic operations, eg formula A1+B1 entered into cell C1 would add the contents of A1 and B1 and put the answer in C1.

Important In calculations across columns in the same row, you can leave out the row number, eg **A/B*100** can be entered in a cell in column **C**.

11.3 Copying a calculation to a number of cells

1 Move your cursor to the cell containing the calculation to be copied.

2 Select **Copy Formula** from the **Maths** option in the **Table Edit** menu.

3 Select **2** or **Down** to copy down a column, or **3** or **Right** to copy to a row.

4 Key in the number of times to copy the formula and Exit to the text.

Activity 4

1 Load up the file **UNIT11-1**, the invoice saved in Activity 3
2 Edit the heading to use it for the invoice below, which has the same layout
3 Save as file **UNIT11-2**
4 Delete the table and set up instead one with 4 columns and 10 rows
5 Enter in the table the Number, Item and Unit Price for each item. Then enter the formula **A*C** in the final column for the first item
6 Copy the formula down for the remaining 4 items, then total the column automatically
7 Remove and set gridlines as shown
8 Preview, save and print

I N V O I C E No **0873**

WELBACK WHOLESALE LTD

112 Forest Road
BRADFORD
W Yorkshire
BD1 8HR

Telephone: 0274 839912
Fax: 0274 856411

Today's date

Mr D Moyer
The Corner Shop
Haworth
W Yorkshire
BD10 5CH

No	Item	Unit Price	Total Price
5	Jar Welback Drinking Chocolate 124 gm	1.18	5.90
20	Jars Welback Coffee Granules 100 gm	1.49	29.80
100	Welback House Tea Bags 60's	1.69	169.00
50	Welback Chocolate Chip Cookies 100 gm	0.34	17.00
50	Hounds Malted Milk 125 gm	0.64	32.00
	TOTAL		£ 247.80

5% Cash Discount for payment on delivery

VAT Registered No 134 6723 43

Further uses

1 Any letter which includes calculations

2 Quotations

3 Simple estimates

Problem solving

- *When you enter the formula for a calculation, you get the answer 0.00.*

  You have not yet entered values in all the cells you are using in the calculation. Enter the values, display the **Table Edit** menu and select **Maths Calculate** to recalculate.

- *The answer to a calculation is displayed as ??.*

  One of the values in your calculation is not a number. Check that you have no spaces before or after the digits, delete them and recalculate, as above.

- *The answer to a calculation is different to that shown.*

  You may have changed a figure since you entered the calculation. Display the **Table Edit** menu and select **Maths Calculate** to recalculate. If this does not solve the problem, you may have entered a formula wrongly. Display the **Table Edit** menu and check the formula. Edit it, if necessary.

- *The tables have gridlines right round them, which looks strange in the middle of an invoice.*

  Remove all gridlines and put in new ones only where required, by selecting a cell or blocks of cells which need gridlines on the same side of them.

- *The fonts and text sizes you have chosen do not look much like the samples.*

  Your fonts depend entirely on the printer you are using. The ones shown are Postscript fonts produced on a laser printer. On a matrix printer, your choices may be much more limited. Select some alternative fonts and preview them to choose the ones you like best.

Unit 12

Meeting notices and agendas

Overview

Not all text fits neatly onto the A4 or standard continuous stationery you have been using so far. You can set up alternative page and paper sizes very easily, and then change between them to suit the job. You can also customise paper size, margins and a number of other page layout features by changing the Initial Codes.

Existing skills

- Copying blocks of text - Unit 2
- Enhancing text - Unit 3
- Changing text size - Unit 4
- Revealing codes - Unit 5
- Using templates - Unit 7
- Setting tabs - Unit 7

New skills

- Setting up special page sizes
- Changing page and paper size
- Changing initial settings
- Combining two files

12.1 Setting up a new paper type

Paper types are a general feature, not related to any particular document. Once a new type has been created, it is available for any document and can also become the default size.

1 Select **Page** from the **Layout** menu to display the **Format: Page** menu.

```
Format: Page
1 - Centre Page (top to bottom)      No
2 - Force Odd/Even Page
3 - Headers
4 - Footers
5 - Margins - Top                    1"
              Bottom                 1"
6 - Page Numbering
7 - Page Size                         8.5" x 11"
         Type                         Standard
8 - Suppress (this page only)
```

2 Select **7** or Page **S**ize/Type to display the **Paper Size/Type** menu.

3 Select **2** or **A**dd to display the **Paper Type** menu and then **9** or **O**ther. Key in a name for the paper type.

4 Select **2** or Paper **S**ize to set the new paper size.

5 Select the appropriate paper size, if it exists, or select **O**ther and type in the dimensions of the new paper size. The new item will be displayed.

6 Select **5** or **L**ocation and choose the paper loading system appropriate for your printer, i.e. **C**ontinuous or **M**anual.

7 Exit to the text. The new type and size is now available for use.

12.2 Selecting a new paper size

1 Display on screen the document which is to use a different paper size.

2 With the cursor at the beginning of the document, display the **Layout Page** menu and select **7** or Paper **S**ize/Type.

3 Highlight the paper size required and choose **1** or **S**elect.

4 Exit to the text.

Activity 1

1 If you have already completed Unit 10 and so have **MEMO.TMP** saved on disk, load it and display on screen

or

If the file is not on disk, key in the memo template shown below, with a tab set at 1.5"

2 Set up a paper type with the standard measurements of 5.83" x 8.27" called **A5**, with the appropriate paper loading option for your printer. *You can print A5 documents on A4 or standard 11" continuous paper for practice*

3 Select this paper type and save the template again, with the same name

```
                    M E M O R A N D U M

Date:

To:

From:

Subject:
----------------------------------------------------------
```

12.3 Changing initial settings

The Initial Codes set defaults such as paper size, language, etc for all future documents. These codes are not normally shown.

1 Select **Setup** from the **File** menu, followed by **Initial Settings**.

2 Select **5** or Initial **C**odes, to display the hidden initial codes in your files.

```
Initial codes Press Exit when finished                Ln 1" Pos 1"
```

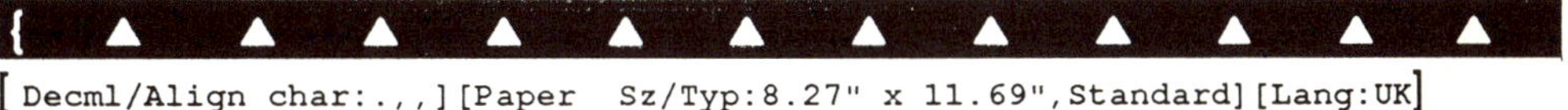

```
[Decml/Align char:.,,][Paper Sz/Typ:8.27" x 11.69",Standard][Lang:UK]
```

3 Use the cursor to highlight and delete the code for Paper size, as when revealing codes.

4 Select **Page** from the **Layout** menu to display the **Format: Page** menu.

5 To change the default page size, choose **Paper Size/Type** and select the Paper Size/Type you want. Its code will be displayed on screen.

6 Make any other changes you want from the menu, then Exit to the text.

12.4 Notices of meeting

Notices for meetings are sent out in advance by the Secretary to those entitled to attend. They may be formal or informal, but must give the minimum information of date, time and venue.

Activity 2

1. Clear the screen, if necessary
2. Change the default paper type/size to A5, the new type set up in Activity 1
3. Change the default left and right margins to .5", a more suitable setting for A5 paper
4. Key in the formal notice of meeting shown below, keeping to the given display
5. Proof read, correct any mistakes, save as **UNIT12-1** and print one copy

PARISH OF WILFORD ON THE WOLDS

NOTICE OF MEETING OF THE PARISH COUNCIL

Dear Sir/Madam

There will be a meeting of the Parish Council at Wilford Village Hall on Monday, 9 March at 7.30 pm.

Dated Monday 2 March

K N Moyse
Clerk of the Parish Council

Activity 3

1. Clear the screen and key in the formal notice of AGM given below, using enhancements as shown
2. Add 3 extra blank lines at the end of the notice
3. Copy and paste the whole notice, with the blank lines, twice more on to the page
4. Preview to check the display and add any extra blank lines needed
5. Save as **UNIT12-2** and print one copy

Formal notice of AGM

THE COUNTRYSIDE CONSERVATION ASSOCIATION

The Annual General Meeting of the Countryside Conservation Association will be held at the Association Head Office, Barton House, Connaught Place, Teddington, Middlesex, on Thursday, 31 March at 1400 hours.

Activity 4

1 Retrieve the memo template saved as **MEMO.TMP** in Activity 1
2 Use it to produce the informal notice of meeting shown below, using tab to line up the items in the heading and generating the date automatically
3 Save as **UNIT12-3**

```
                    M E M O R A N D U M

Date:       Today's date

To:         Midlands Sales Staff

From:       Sales Director (Midlands)

Subject:    Sales Meeting

----------------------------------------------------------

There will be a meeting of all Midlands sales staff at
Soar House, New Road, Leicester, on Wednesday, 12 March,
at 1000 hours.
```

12.5 Agenda layout

There is a standard layout for a meeting agenda, which is made up of standard items of business, 1-3, 9 and 10 in the sample, together with additional items specific to the particular organisation and meeting. It is, therefore, worth having an agenda template.

AGENDA

1 Apologies
2 Minutes of last meeting
3 Matters arising
4)
5)
6) Specific subjects
7)
8)
9 Any other business
10 Date and time of next meeting

Activity 5

1 Clear the screen, if necessary, and select the Paper size/type A4 single sheet or 11" Continuous, depending on your printer
2 Check your margins and change them back to 1" either side, if necessary
3 Key in the agenda template
4 Check and save as **AGENDA.TMP**

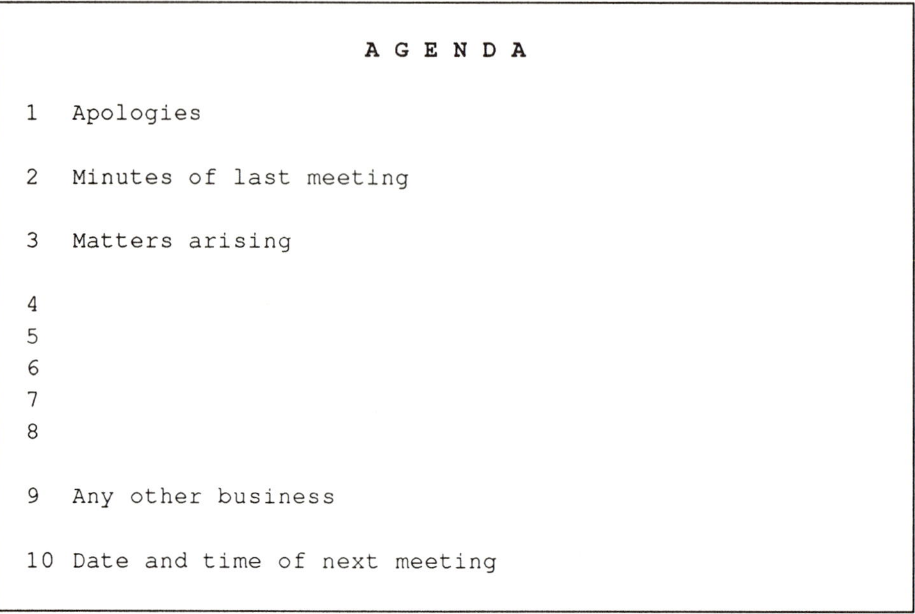

A G E N D A

1 Apologies

2 Minutes of last meeting

3 Matters arising

4
5
6
7
8

9 Any other business

10 Date and time of next meeting

12.6 Combining two files

When you want 2 existing files to be joined together to form one document, which flows on continuously, you can combine them very easily.

1 With a clear screen, retrieve the first file in the usual way to display it on screen.

2 Move the cursor to the position in the document where the second file is to start, often either the beginning or end of the first file.

3 Retrieve the second file. It will be read in, beginning at the cursor position.

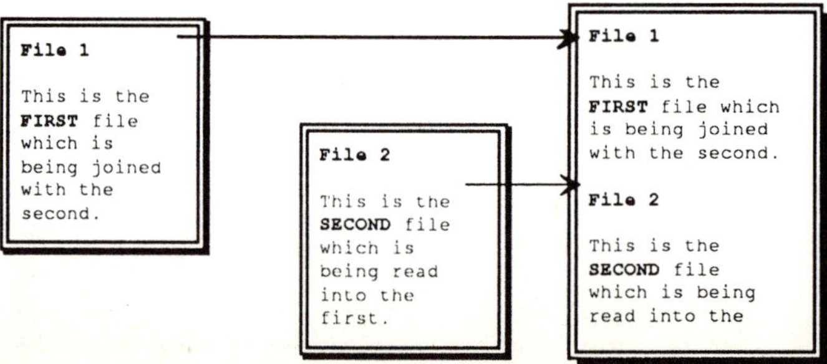

File 1
This is the FIRST file which is being joined with the second.
File 2
This is the SECOND file which is being read into the first.
File 1
This is the FIRST file which is being joined with the second.
File 2
This is the SECOND file which is being read into the

Activity 6

1 As a notice of meeting and the relevant agenda are usually sent out together, these 2 files can to be combined to fit on one page
2 Retrieve the agenda template saved as **AGENDA.TMP** in Activity 5
3 Complete the agenda for a meeting of the Midland Sales Staff by adding the following items of business:
   4 Business review
   5 Targets
   6 Promotions
   7 Visits
   8 Street food analysis
   9 New product launch
4 Save as **UNIT12-4**, ie a new name so that the template still exists for other purposes
5 Read in the notice of meeting saved as **UNIT12-3** in Activity 4, to create a combined document
6 Check and preview, and select A4 or 11" continuous paper, depending on your printer
7 Save again and print

```
                    M E M O R A N D U M

Date:       5 March 19xx

To:         Midlands Sales Staff

From:       Sales Director (Midlands)

Subject:    Sales Meeting
----------------------------------------------------------

There will be a meeting of all Midlands sales staff at
Soar House, New Road, Leicester, on Wednesday, 12 March,
at 1000 hours.
                         A G E N D A

1  Apologies
2  Minutes of last meeting
3  Matters arising
4  Business review
5  Targets
6  Promotions
7  Visits
8  Street food analysis
9  New product launch
10 Any other business
11 Date and time of next meeting
```

Further uses

1 Quotations

2 Extracting facts from another file for a letter

3 Laying out A5 booklets

Problem solving

- *Even though you are using continuous stationery, only one page is printed.*

  You have not set the **Location** to Continuous when setting up your new paper size. The default setting is **Manual**, so the printer is waiting for you to insert paper and give the signal to print the next page. Select **Print** from the **File** menu, followed by **Control Printer**. You will see a message telling you to press **G** to start printing. Do so, then after printing, change the paper definition to reflect your continuous stationery.

- *The agenda and notice of meeting do not follow on from each other, but are interleaved.*

  Your cursor was at the wrong place in your document before you retrieved the second file. Clear the screen, load up the agenda again in its edited form, move your cursor to the end and retrieve the notice of meeting again.

- *Your paper size has not been used in previewing and printing a new file.*

  You may have set up the new paper size only in the current document, rather than as part of the Initial Settings. Follow the procedure to change the Initial Settings.

Unit 13

Chair's agenda

Overview

In order to give a consistent look to your text, which is particularly important for documents which run over several pages, you can set up Styles. A style is a set of features which specify the appearance of any word or piece of text which has that style applied to it.

Existing skills

- Aligning text - Unit 4
- Changing text size - Unit 4
- Setting Initial Codes - Unit 12

New skills

- Creating styles
- Saving and retrieving style files

Important Possible styles depend entirely on your printer. Matrix printers may have a Sans Serif and a Serif font (*see* Unit 11) in a number of fixed sizes, measured in characters per inch (cpi). Laser printers, and any printer being used with Windows, will provide a wider range of fonts measured in points (72 points = 1 inch). Twelve cpi is approximately the same size as 10 point, so these alternatives are used in each activity.

The following features are usually set in styles:

- Font type and size
- Appearance ie underlining, emboldening, etc
- Alignment

Styles also need a name which is used for selection. The name should be chosen to prompt its use, eg Heading, Side heading, List.

13.1 Creating a style

1. Select **Styles** from the **Layout** menu, followed by **3** or **C**reate to set up a new style through the **Styles Edit** menu.
2. Select **1** or **N**ame and enter a name for the style to remind you.
3. Select **3** or **D**escription and key in a short description.

```
Styles: Edit

1 - Name
2 - Type                Paired
3 - Description
4 - Codes
5 - Enter               HRt
```

4. Select **4** or **C**odes to display a screen similar to that used to set Initial Codes (*see* Unit 12). Choose Base Font and Size features from the **Font** menu and Alignment or Justification from the **Layout** menu. If you want bold text, you need to enter **F6** both above and below the line indicated.

Activity 1

1. If you have already completed Unit 12 and so have **UNIT12-4** saved on disk, load it, display on screen and delete all but the Agenda heading and numbered items. Insert a blank line between each item. Set tabs at .25", 4" and 4.25"

   or

   If the file is not on disk, key in the agenda shown below and set the tabs as above
2. Create 3 styles as follows, with suitable descriptions:

   Centre head - centred, sans serif 12 point/10 cpi, very large text and bold

   Side head - left justified, sans serif 10 point/12 cpi, large text and bold

   Body text - left justified, serif 10 point/12 cpi
3. Save the file, with the styles, as **UNIT13-1**

```
1  Apologies

2  Minutes of last meeting

3  Matters arising

4  Business Review

5  Targets

6  Promotions

7  Visits

8  Street food analysis

9  New product launch

10 Any other business

11 Date and time of next meeting
```

13.2 Applying styles to text

1. Before entering text, or after highlighting text to which the style is to be applied, select **Styles** from the **Layout** menu.
2. Highlight the style required and select **1** or **O**n.
3. For styles which need turning off, with the cursor at the end of the text, select **L**ayout **S**tyles Off.

13.3 Saving styles to use with other documents

1. Select **Styles** from the **Layout** menu.
2. Select **6** or **S**ave and enter a filename for the styles. All those attached to the document will be saved to the file.
3. When you have loaded a file, display the **Styles** menu, select **R**etrieve and enter the name of the styles file to use them with the new file.

Activity 2

1. Load up **UNIT13-1** which was saved with its accompanying styles in Activity 1
2. Use the tab settings to add the comments to the agenda for the Chair
3. Apply Centre Head style to the edited heading, Side Heading style to the numbers and agenda items and Body text to the comments
4. Save the styles as **STYLES**, preview the display, save the agenda and print

CHAIR'S AGENDA

1 Apologies	1 Tod Crisp/Helen Danvers
2 Minutes of last meeting	2 Sign
3 Matters arising	
4 Business Review	3 Present charts and graphs
5 Targets	4 Tam Wyatt
6 Promotions	6 Details from Kelly Jay
7 Visits	7 Individual reports
8 Street food analysis	8 Statistics
9 New product launch	9 Take samples 'Panther'
10 Any other business	
11 Date and time of next meeting	11 Allow one month - to be held in Nottingham

Further uses

1 Reports (*see* Unit 17)

2 Newsletters (*see* Unit 21)

3 Any document which requires consistent display

Problem solving

- *Your text does not look like the samples.*

  You may just have a different set of fonts available. The samples were produced on a laser printer using Helvetica. Your sans serif font may look quite different.

- *Even though you are using continuous stationery, only one page is printed.*

  You did not set the **Location** to Continuous when setting up your new paper size. The default setting is **Manual**, so the printer is waiting for you to insert paper and give the signal to print the next page. Select **Print** from the **File** menu, followed by **Control Printer**. You will see a message telling you to press **G** to start printing. Do so, then after printing, change the paper definition to reflect your continuous stationery.

- *The correct paper size has not been used in previewing and printing the file.*

  If you have not already completed Unit 12, you will not have set up a new paper size. Follow the procedure given in Unit 12 to set a new paper size and to change the Initial Settings to use it.

Unit 14

Minutes

Objectives In all the units so far, the text has fitted neatly onto one page, either A4, 11" continuous stationery or A5. In reality, many documents take up more than one page. It is in formatting pages that word processing really comes into its own, as quite major changes can be accomplished with a few key strokes.

Existing skills

- Indenting paragraphs - Unit 5
- Setting tabs - Unit 7
- Using styles - Unit 13

New skills

- Setting up headers and footers
- Editing headers and footers
- Numbering pages
- Printing selected pages
- Splitting pages at convenient points in text

Important Headers and footers are lines of text which appear on every page, or on all even or odd pages, if you prefer. They usually contain items such as file names, date and time, chapter headings in books, and most usefully, page numbers.

14.1 Setting up a header or footer

1 With the cursor at the beginning of the file, select **Page** from the **Layout** menu, followed by **Headers** or **Footers**.

2 Select **1** or Header **A** (Footer **A** for footer), then **2** or Every **P**age, to enter the first header or footer of a possible two, to be displayed on all pages, including the first.

3 Enter the text for the header or footer on the editing screen displayed, using the menus to align and change the font or appearance of the text. Then exit to the text.

14.2 Numbering pages

1 Select **Page** from the **Layout** menu, followed by **Page numbering**.

2 Select **4** or Page Number **P**osition to display the page numbering diagrams.

3 Key in the number of the position and display you want, eg keying **7** will set a page number right justified in the footer on every page.

4 The position chosen will be displayed on the menu. Exit to the text.

Activity 1

1 If you have already completed Unit 13 and so have **UNIT13-1** saved on disk with its associated styles, load it, display on screen and delete the comments
or
If the file is not on disk, you will need to set up the styles specified in Activity 1 of Unit 13
Key in the agenda shown below, applying Centre Head style to the heading and Side Heading style to the numbers and agenda items

2 Save as **UNIT14-1**

AGENDA

1 Apologies
2 Minutes of last meeting
3 Matters arising
4 Business Review
5 Targets
6 Promotions
7 Visits
8 Street food analysis
9 New product launch
10 Any other business
11 Date and time of next meeting

Activity 2

1 Load up the outline agenda saved as **UNIT14-1** in Activity 1
2 Using the agenda headings, key in the minutes given on this and the following 2 pages, using styles as shown
3 Check the spelling, preview and save
4 Print one copy on A4 or 11" continuous stationery

MINUTES

Minutes of a meeting of Midlands Sales Staff at Soar House, New Road, Leicester, on Wednesday, 12 March 19.., at 1000 hours.

Present

Michael Schaal (Chairman)	Chris Booth
Carol Breedon	Kelly Jay
Mike Oates	Judy Prior
Tina Salami	Anne Simpson
Nat Singh	Paul Ure
Jo Van Gyseghem	Brad West
Tam Wyatt	Mel Winters (Secretary)

1 Apologies

Apologies were received from Tod Crisp and Helen Danvers.

2 Minutes of last meeting

The minutes of the last meeting, which had been circulated, were confirmed as a true record and signed by the Chairman.

3 Matters arising

Paul Ure reported that all his attempts at retaining the key account with Macedon's Stores had proved abortive. The Chairman said that he would have a word with him on the subject after the meeting.

4 Business review

The Chairman presented charts and graphs showing the present position in the Midlands. The Company was 37% below target in the present financial year; the area 19% below. The Chairman was pleased to note that the area was performing significantly better than the national trends and was certain that a small surplus could be made at the year end in December. Sales of boxed chocolates and chocolate bars had fallen considerably and this would be one of the topics of discussion at the next meeting. He said that, overall, the picture was gloomy and great efforts would have to be made by the entire Midlands sales force in order to reverse the trend. In response to questions, he acknowledged that poor trade was a reflection of the current economic climate.

5 Targets

Tam Wyatt circulated copies of the February sales results. The Chairman congratulated Tina Salami on achieving top sales and said that she had become a valuable team member.

6 Promotions

Kelly Jay presented the promotions planned in April. These were aimed at the health bar market and included 2 nut and fruit bar promotions of 'Nutbic'- 'Buy five - get one free'.

It was intended to consolidate the street food promotions by providing a flash pack reducing 'Slick' bars from 24p each to 19p.

Due to the flagging sales of the family chocolate bar, there would be a promotion on the Golden bar range offering a 10p money-back coupon on next purchase.
Sales promotional materials, samples and dump bins were provided for sales people to collect at the end of the meeting.

7 Visits

Individual reports on sales visits were presented by the 4 Sales Managers:

Jo Van Gyseghem
Judy Prior
Anne Simpson
Brad West

The Chairman congratulated the Managers on the enthusiasm and dedication of themselves and their staff and urged them on to even greater efforts.

8 Street food analysis

Market research reports showed that the chocolate bar which could be eaten in the street was still popular although sales overall were affected by the current diet trend. Low calorie foods were selling well and new products would be aimed at that market; namely diet street food.

9 New product launch

The Chairman announced that the new chocolate bar 'Panther' would be launched in May. Technical problems had caused the delay. Tasting samples in all 4 flavours were circulated and bulk supplies would be available after the meeting. Sales people should use promotional and merchandising materials distributed at the December conference. The publicity had been widespread and the product should do well.

10 Any other business

10.1 **Company Cars** Nat Singh asked if the Chairman knew of any change in policy on company cars. The Chairman replied that he had heard various rumours circulating but these were without foundation and there was no change in policy.

10.2 **Redundancies** Carol Breedon asked if there was any truth in the rumour regarding redundancies in the firm as a whole. The Chairman said that some cut backs would be necessary but that it was hoped to achieve these by natural wastage; no redundancies were planned at this time.

10.3 **Charities** Chris Booth suggested that a promotion should be launched whereby a small percentage was donated to charity. The Chairman asked the Secretary to place this on the agenda for the next meeting.

11 Date and time of next meeting

The next meeting would be held at the Nottingham offices at 1000 hours, on Wednesday, 8 April.

Activity 3

1. Load up the minutes, saved as **UNIT14-1** in Activity 2
2. Set up a one line footer in small size text for every page of the document as follows:
   Left hand margin - *British Chocolates plc*
   Centred - automatic date
3. Put in a page number at the bottom right hand margin
4. Set up a one line header in small size text for every page as follows:
   Centred - *Minutes - Midland Sales Staff*
   Right justified - *Wednesday 12 March*
5. Preview to make sure that the header and footer have been correctly set up and are displayed on each page

14.3 Editing a header or footer

1. Select **Page** from the **Layout** menu, followed by **Header A** or **Footer A** and select **5** or Edit.

2. Your header or footer wil be displayed on the codes screen. Edit it in the usual way and Exit to the text.

14.4 Ending pages

Page ends are shown by a hoizontal line across the screen and are generated automatically by WordPerfect when you have entered the number of lines which fill the current page size. You may want to end a page sooner than this, to keep text together with its heading, for example.

1 Move the cursor to the beginning of the line where the new page is to begin.

2 Hold down the Ctrl key and press **Return** to insert a hard page code. You can see the code **[HPg]** if you Reveal Codes.

3 If you change your mind about the page end, you can use Backspace to delete the code, or Reveal Codes to do so.

14.5 Printing selected pages

1 Load up the file which is to be printed to display it on screen.

2 Move your cursor to any position in the page you wish to print.

3 Select **Print** from the **File** menu and select **2** or **P**age.

4 The current page will be printed.

Activity 3

1 Load up the minutes saved as **UNIT14-1**

2 Add blank lines after each heading and use **Layout Align Indent** to indent the main text under each heading, as shown below

> **1 Apologies**
>
> Apologies were received from Tod Crisp and Helen Danvers.
>
> **2 Minutes of last meeting**
>
> The minutes of the last meeting, which had been circulated, were confirmed as a true record and signed by the Chairman.

3 Edit the header to be displayed as shown below, using Reveal Codes to change alignment

Midland Sales Staff   12 March 19xx

4 Preview to check the heading and save, before continuing with the editing

Activity 4

1 Set an additional tab at .75", before section 10 of the minutes, and indent the sub-sections to the second tab, as shown below

> **10 Any other business**
>
> **10.1 Company Cars** Nat Singh asked if the Chairman knew of any change in policy on company cars. The Chairman replied that he had heard various rumours circulating but these were without foundation and there was no change in policy.
>
> **10.2 Redundancies** Carol Breedon asked if there was any truth in the rumour regarding redundancies in the firm as a whole. The Chairman said that some cut backs would be necessary but that it was hoped to achieve these by natural wastage; no redundancies were planned at this time.
>
> **10.3 Charities** Chris Booth suggested that a promotion should be launched whereby a small percentage was donated to charity. The Chairman asked the Secretary to place this on the agenda for the next meeting.

2 Move through the document from beginning to end, putting in page breaks where required to keep complete items with their heading, ie page breaks should be immediately *before* a heading

3 Print the third page, to check the layout and the header and footer and save again

Important You may sometimes want to fit a multi-page document onto fewer pages, for example to make photocopying cheaper. The easiest way to do this is to reduce the size of the main text, particularly if you are using styles. All you have to do is to edit your Body Text style; the document will be re-formatted automatically to fit the new size.

Activity 5

1 Load up the minutes again

2 Take out the page breaks you put in, as they will be inappropriate when the text size has been changed

3 Edit the Body Text style to use 8 point or 15 cpi, whichever is available on your printer

4 Preview the document, then insert a page break, if necessary

5 Save and print. Your document should look like the sample document shown on the next 2 pages

Midland Sales Staff 12 March 19xx

MINUTES

Minutes of a meeting of Midlands Sales Staff at Soar House, New Road, Leicester, on Wednesday, 12 March 19.., at 1000 hours.

Present

Michael Schaal (Chairman)
Carol Breedon
Mike Oates
Tina Salami
Nat Singh
Jo Van Gyseghem
Tam Wyatt
Chris Booth
Kelly Jay
Judy Prior
Anne Simpson
Paul Ure
Brad West
Mel Winters (Secretary)

1 Apologies

Apologies were received from Tod Crisp and Helen Danvers.

2 Minutes of last meeting

The minutes of the last meeting, which had been circulated, were confirmed as a true record and signed by the Chairman.

3 Matters arising

Paul Ure reported that all his attempts at retaining the key account with Macedon's Stores had proved abortive. The Chairman said that he would have a word with him on the subject after the meeting.

4 Business review

The Chairman presented charts and graphs showing the present position in the Midlands. The Company was 37% below target in the present financial year; the area 19% below. The Chairman was pleased to note that the area was performing significantly better than the national trends and was certain that a small surplus could be made at the year end in December. Sales of boxed chocolates and chocolate bars had fallen considerably and this would be one of the topics of discussion at the next meeting. He said that, overall, the picture was gloomy and great efforts would have to be made by the entire Midlands sales force in order to reverse the trend. In response to questions, he acknowledged that poor trade was a reflection of the current economic climate.

5 Targets

Tam Wyatt circulated copies of the February sales results. The Chairman congratulated Tina Salami on achieving top sales and said that she had become a valuable team member.

6 Promotions

Kelly Jay presented the promotions planned in April. These were aimed at the health bar market and included 2 nut and fruit bar promotions of 'Nutbic'- 'Buy five - get one free'.

It was intended to consolidate the street food promotions by providing a flash pack reducing 'Slick' bars from 24p each to 19p.

Due to the flagging sales of the family chocolate bar, there would be a promotion on the Golden bar range offering a 10p money-back coupon on next purchase.

Sales promotional materials, samples and dump bins were provided for sales people to collect at the end of the meeting.

British Chocolates plc 2 May 19xx 1

Midland Sales Staff 12 March 19xx

7 Visits

Individual reports on sales visits were presented by the 4 Sales Managers:

Jo Van Gyseghem
Judy Prior
Anne Simpson
Brad West

The Chairman congratulated the Managers on the enthusiasm and dedication of themselves and their staff and urged them on to even greater efforts.

8 Street food analysis

Market research reports showed that the chocolate bar which could be eaten in the street was still popular although sales overall were affected by the current diet trend. Low calorie foods were selling well and new products would be aimed at that market; namely diet street food.

9 New product launch

The Chairman announced that the new chocolate bar 'Panther' would be launched in May. Technical problems had caused the delay. Tasting samples in all 4 flavours were circulated and bulk supplies would be available after the meeting. Sales people to use promotional and merchandising materials distributed at the December conference. The publicity had been widespread and the product should do well.

10 Any other business

10.1 **Company Cars** Nat Singh asked if the Chairman knew of any change in policy on company cars. The Chairman replied that he had heard various rumours circulating but these were without foundation and there was no change in policy.

10.2 **Redundancies** Carol Breedon asked if there was any truth in the rumour regarding redundancies in the firm as a whole. The Chairman said that some cut backs would be necessary but that it was hoped to achieve these by natural wastage; no redundancies were planned at this time.

10.3 **Charities** Chris Booth suggested that a promotion should be launched whereby a small percentage was donated to charity. The Chairman asked the Secretary to place this on the agenda for the next meeting.

11 Date and time of next meeting

The next meeting would be held at the Nottingham offices at 1000 hours, on Wednesday, 8 April.

British Chocolates plc 2 May 19xx 2

Further uses

1 Any multi-page document

2 Books and articles

3 Reports (*see* Unit 17)

4 Newletters (*see* Unit 21)

Problem solving

- *Only the first page of the minutes is printed, when you asked for the full document to be printed.*

  Your paper type includes manual feed. Select **File Page** followed by **Control Printer** to display the **Print: Control Printer** menu. A message will be displayed asking you to press **G** to start printing. Insert paper, if necessary and press **G** to print the next page. Repeat for each page.

- *The text is printed across the perforation on continuous stationery.*

  You did not set the top of page setting on your printer before you started. Set top of page according to the printer manual (usually pressing a button) or re-load the paper, and print again.

- *Your document does not fit on the same number of pages as in the example.*

  The spacing set for your printer is probably slightly different from the laser printer used to produce the sample. Reduce the size of your text still further, if this is possible, or use slightly smaller left and right margins.

- *Even though you have reset the top of the page on your printer, the pages do not fit on A4 single sheet paper; a little bit has to be printed on the next sheet.*

  Your printer may be set to leave a margin before it starts to print. You may be able to set the **printer's** top margin to be very small - you will need to refer to the manual.

- *When using single sheets, the printer stops before the bottom of the page is printed and asks for another sheet.*

  The printer's paper sensor reports that there is no paper before the bottom of the page, as it is positioned on the bottom of the roller. Set a larger bottom margin on your page size to deal with this. You may need to experiment to get this right.

Unit 15

Mailmerge

Overview There are many circumstances in which you may want to produce personalised letters to be sent to a large number of individuals or firms. WordPerfect can help you to do this automatically.

Existing skills

- Business letter layout - Unit 6
- Automatic date - Unit 6
- Tabs - Unit 7

New skills

- Setting up data as a secondary file for variable details
- Setting up a letter as a primary file for mailmerge
- Inserting variable details to produce a personalised letter

Important You may need to split up your data into a number of separate items, in order to use it in a number of different ways, eg postcodes often need to be separate, as do the separate parts of names.

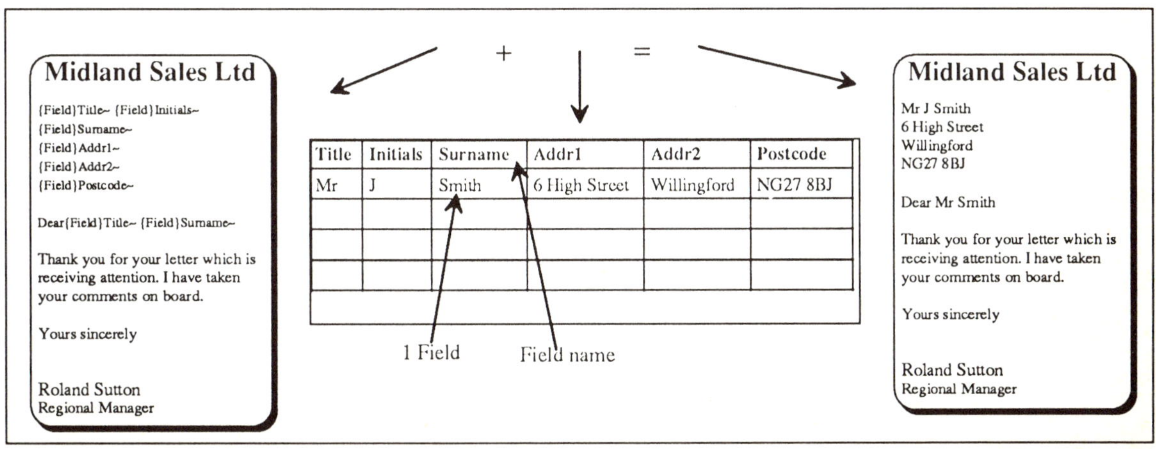

Midland Sales Ltd
{Field}Title~ {Field}Initials~
{Field}Surname~
{Field}Addr1~
{Field}Addr2~
{Field}Postcode~
Dear{Field}Title~ {Field}Surname~
Thank you for your letter which is receiving attention. I have taken your comments on board.
Yours sincerely
Roland Sutton
Regional Manager
+
=
Title | Initials | Surname | Addr1 | Addr2 | Postcode
Mr | J | Smith | 6 High Street | Willingford | NG27 8BJ
1 Field
Field name
Midland Sales Ltd
Mr J Smith
6 High Street
Willingford
NG27 8BJ
Dear Mr Smith
Thank you for your letter which is receiving attention. I have taken your comments on board.
Yours sincerely
Roland Sutton
Regional Manager

15.1 Setting up data as a secondary file

To merge data, you use a special type of file which contains only the variable information. The data in this file is made up of records, each containing a set of information about one person, split into fields. It is best to set this up before creating the main file which is to have the variables added to it. One data file is, in any case, likely to be used with a number of main files.

1 Clear the screen, if necessary.

2 Select **Merge Codes** from the **Tools** menu, followed by **More**.

3 Select the option **{FIELD NAMES}name1~...nameN~~** from the list of merge codes displayed.

4 At the message *Enter Field 1*, key in the name of the first field, e.g. title and press **Return**. Continue to key in each field name as prompted. After the last field name has been entered, press **Return** twice to end.

5 The complete field name definition will be displayed at the top of the file. This line forms the description for the records in the file.

6 Type in the data for the first record, pressing **F9** to insert the {END FIELD} code at the end of each field. Leave blank any field which does not have an entry for a particular individual, but put in the {END FIELD} code. All the records must have the same number of fields. There should be no blank lines between fields.

7 After all the fields have been entered, select **Merge Codes** from the **Tools** menu, followed by **End Record**, to enter the code {END RECORD}, which also generates the double line to end the record.

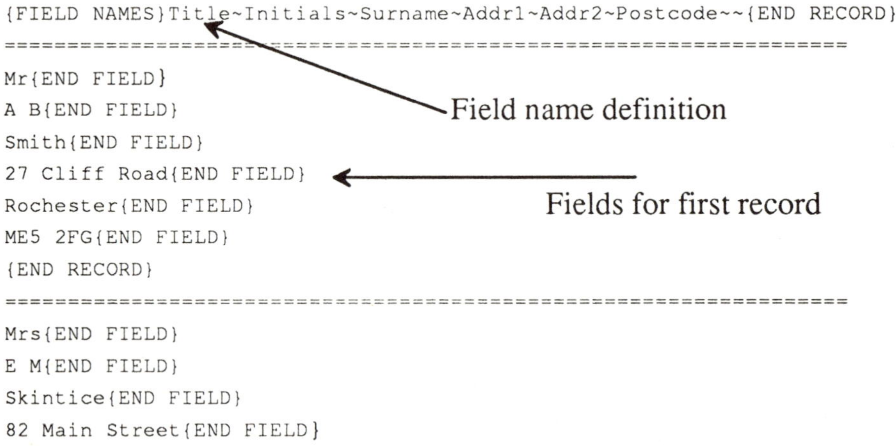

```
{FIELD NAMES}Title~Initials~Surname~Addr1~Addr2~Postcode~~{END RECORD}
=====================================================================
Mr{END FIELD}
A B{END FIELD}
Smith{END FIELD}
27 Cliff Road{END FIELD}
Rochester{END FIELD}
ME5 2FG{END FIELD}
{END RECORD}
=====================================================================
Mrs{END FIELD}
E M{END FIELD}
Skintice{END FIELD}
82 Main Street{END FIELD}
```


8 Key in the rest of the records, in the same way, and save the file to disk.

Activity 1

1 Set up a new data file called **CUSTOMER.DAT**, with fields Title, Initials, Surname, Addr1, Addr2, Addr3, Postcode
2 Enter the following customer details into it, being sure to split up the elements of the names, so that they can be used in the address and after *Dear*
3 Save the file and print a copy for reference

```
Mr C Able
56 Mere Green
COVENTRY
CV1 2HF

Miss N Brightwell
114 London Road
COVENTRY
CV1 5HF

Mrs C Ferrell
Flat 1A
Valley Road
COVENTRY
CV2 8TB

Mr I Rachins
98 Templeton Road
COVENTRY
CV2 9TB

Mr N Shaw
3 Court Place
The Park
COVENTRY
CV1 7HF

C M Barry
Church Croft
COVENTRY
CV10 2LR
```

15.2 Setting up the main file

1 Clear the screen, if necessary.

2 Key in the document as normal, but whenever you reach a point where an item of variable data is required, insert a field code in the following way.

3 Select **Merge Codes** from the **Tools** menu, followed by **Field**.

4 At the message *Enter Field:*, key in the name of the field you require. The code {FIELD} followed by the field name and the ~ symbol will be inserted in the file, as shown in the example. It is important to insert spaces between the fields in the first line, as this is how they need to be printed.

```
{FIELD}Title~ {FIELD}Initials~ {FIELD}Surname~
{FIELD}Addr1~
{FIELD}Addr2~
{FIELD}Addr3~
{FIELD}Postcode~
```

5 Save the file to disk for later use.

Activity 2

1 Key in the following letter, generating the date automatically
2 Insert the fields from the data file **CUSTOMER.DAT** set up in Activity 1, as shown
3 Proof read on screen and save to disk as **LETTER.DOC**
4 Print a reference copy

```
Today's date

{FIELD}Title~ {FIELD}Initials~ {FIELD}Surname~
{FIELD}Addr1~
{FIELD}Addr2~
{FIELD}Addr3~
{FIELD}Postcode~

Dear {FIELD}Title~ {FIELD}Surname~

I hope that you have enjoyed many miles of trouble free
motoring since you bought your car from Arthur Swan of
Coventry.

Although at the time of purchase you did not take up the
option of the extended warranty available for second and
third year parts and labour cover, it is not too late.

If you have reconsidered and would now like to take
advantage of the offer which could bring you another 2
year's motoring with the consequent peace of mind, please
contact Richard Lister on 0203 566321.

Yours sincerely




RICHARD LISTER
Business Manager
```

15.3 Merging two files

1. Clear the screen, if necessary and select **Merge** from the **Tools** menu.
2. At the prompt *Primary file:* key in the name of the main file you have created, ie the one which contains the letter.
3. At the next prompt *Secondary file:* key in the name of the data file, ie the file which contains the names and addresses.
4. The letters will be merged and the finished letters displayed on screen.
5. Proof read on screen, check the printer is ready and print one copy, inserting additional sheets of paper, if required.

Activity 3

1. Use the files **LETTER1** and **CUSTOMER.DTA** to produce the 6 letters required
2. Check that the first one comes out like the specimen shown below

```
Today's date

Mr C Able
56 Mere Green
COVENTRY
CV1 2HF

Dear Mr Able

I hope that you have enjoyed many miles of trouble free
motoring since you bought your car from Arthur Swan of
Coventry.

Although at the time of purchase you did not take up the
option of the extended warranty available for second and
third year parts and labour cover, it is not too late.

If you have reconsidered and would now like to take
advantage of the offer which could bring you another 2
year's motoring with the consequent peace of mind, please
contact Richard Lister on 0203 566321.

Yours sincerely




RICHARD LISTER
Business Manager
```

Further uses

1 Producing automatic labels (*see* Unit 16)

2 Producing personalised invitations

3 Any mailshot

Problem solving

- *There are no spaces between the separate parts of the names in the letter, either in the name and address section, or after Dear .*

  You did not press the space bar between fields to give the required spacing in the primary file. Retrieve the primary file, if necessary, and put in the extra spaces.

- *One of your letters has jumbled fields, eg Miss 114 London Road.*

  You have missed out a field in this record in your data file, making all the rest move up to fill the space. Check your data file to make sure that all 7 fields are present in every record, even when one is blank.

- *You are using single sheets of paper and only one letter has been printed.*

  The printer may be waiting for another sheet of paper, so you may need to load one. Select **Print** from the **File** menu, followed by **Control Printer**. You will see a message telling you to press **G** to start printing once you have loaded the paper.

- *Even though you are using continuous stationery, only one page is printed.*

  You have not set the **Location** to Continuous when setting up your new paper size. The default setting is **Manual**, so the printer is waiting for you to insert paper and give the signal to print the next page. Select **Print** from the **File** menu, followed by **Control Printer**. You will see a message telling you to press **G** to start printing. Do so, then after printing, change the paper definition to reflect your continuous stationery.

Unit 16

Labels and envelopes

Overview

Once you have a file of names and addresses, you can use them for several purposes, including producing labels automatically for the letters you have mailmerged, and for printing directly onto envelopes.

Existing skills

- Changing page and paper size - Unit 12
- Setting up a primary file for mailmerge - Unit 15
- Setting up a data file - Unit 15

New skills

- Setting up a page and paper size for labels
- To produce labels automatically
- To print directly to envelopes

Important

You will have to measure the labels you are actually using, to set their measurements, as there are considerable variations in sizes and in the numbers mounted on a page or continuous sheet.

If you are using single sheet labels on a laser printer, then remember that most lasers cannot print closer than 0.5" to each edge. Similarly, if you are loading single sheets into a matrix or inkjet printer by hand, without a single sheet feeder, you will not be able to print very close to the top or bottom of the page.

It is always worth trying out label printing on blank paper before loading labels. They are relatively expensive!

16.1 Creating a customised label paper size

There is a special set of menus for creation of label paper sizes, because there is more than one label on a sheet. There are usually at least 8 on a page, and there may be 24 or more on continuous stationery, in 3 columns.

1. Follow the usual procedure for setting up a new paper size and type, ie select **P**age from the **L**ayout menu, followed by Paper **S**ize/Type to display the relevant menu.
2. Select **A**dd and then **4** or **L**abels and **8** or **L**abels followed by **Y**es to display the **Format: Labels** screen.
3. Set the sizes of your labels, using the diagram below as a guide to the measurements you need.

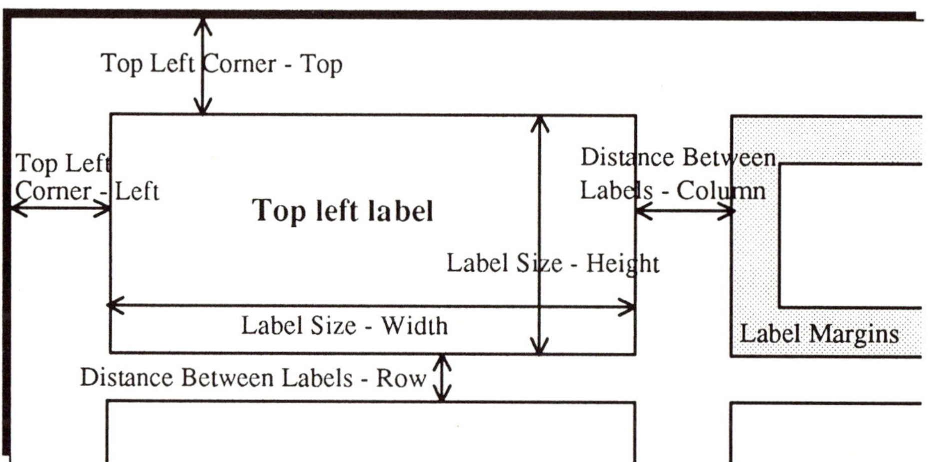

4. Exit to the text to save the new paper size, selecting it immediately, if required.

16.2 Printing labels

1. Set up a secondary file for your label data (*see* Unit 15) and save to disk.
2. Set up a file which contains only fields and any information which you want to appear on every label, eg Training Manager for a mailshot to firms. Make sure that you do not use too many lines for your label.
3. Change the initial codes for the primary file to include the label page definition and save to disk.
4. Use the **Merge** command to produce the labels.

Activity 1

1 If you have completed Unit 15, and so have the file **CUSTOMER.DAT** saved on disk, retrieve it and add the 6 additional names and addresses to it
or
Set up a new data file called **CUSTOMER.DAT**, with fields Title, Initials, Surname, Addr1, Addr2, Addr3, Postcode (*see* Unit 15)
Enter the following customer details into it, being sure to split up the elements of the names into the correct fields
2 Proofread the file on screen, particularly the postcodes. Spell checking is not appropriate, as few of the words used would be in the dictionary
3 Save the file and print a copy for reference

```
Mr C Able
56 Mere Green
COVENTRY
CV1 2HF

Miss N Brightwell
114 London Road
COVENTRY
CV1 5HF

Mrs C Ferrell
Flat 1A
Valley Road
COVENTRY
CV2 8TB

Mr I Rachins
98 Templeton Road
COVENTRY
CV2 9TB

Mr N Shaw
3 Court Place
The Park
COVENTRY
CV1 7HF

C M Barry
Church Croft
COVENTRY
CV10 2LR

Mr J Adcock
75 Springfield Road
COVENTRY
CV1 5HP

Mr K Douglas
103 Stafford Way
COVENTRY
CV22 4JN

Mr S Patel
49 Tandy Road
COVENTRY
CV2 7TB

Miss R Koscina
4 The Grove
COVENTRY
CV3 2BN

Ms C Viharo
43 Hunter's Cross
Bell Green
COVENTRY
CV1 9FH

A B Smith
23 Rectory Road
The Park
COVENTRY
CV1 8XJ
```

Activity 2

1 Clear the screen and set up a new page definition, with the following specification:

OPTION	SETTING
Page size	8.5" x 11" - American Standard continuous stationery
Label size	3.5" wide x 1.45" high
Number	2 columns, 7 rows
Distance between	Column 0", Row 0.05"
Label margins	0.3" on each side, top and bottom

2 Exit to the text and put the new page definition into the initial codes using **Document** from the **Layout** menu, followed by **Initial Codes** (*see* problem-solving)

3 Key in the following text, which consists entirely of field names from the data file **CUSTOMER.DAT**, separated with spaces and Returns

```
{FIELD}Title~ {FIELD}Initials~ {FIELD}Surname~
{FIELD}Addr1~
{FIELD}Addr2~
{FIELD}Addr3~    {FIELD}Postcode~
```
(*4 spaces*)

4 Save as the file **LABEL.TMP**

5 Clear the screen, if necessary and produce the labels by merging the files **LABEL.TMP** (Primary file) and **CUSTOMER.DAT** (Secondary file)

6 Preview to check the display and print on plain paper

Mr C Able
56 Mere Green

COVENTRY CV1 2HF

Miss N Brightwell
114 London Road

COVENTRY CV1 5HF

Mrs C Ferrell
Flat 1A
Valley Road
COVENTRY CV2 8TB

Mr I Rachins
98 Templeton Road

COVENTRY CV2 9TB

Mr N Shaw
3 Court Place
The Park
COVENTRY CV1 7HF

C M Barry
Church Croft

COVENTRY CV10 2LR

Mr J Adcock
75 Springfield Road

COVENTRY CV1 5HP

Mr K Douglas
103 Stafford Way

COVENTRY CV22 4JN

Mr S Patel
49 Tandy Road

COVENTRY CV2 7TB

Miss R Koscina
4 The Grove

COVENTRY CV3 2BN

Ms C Viharo
43 Hunter's Cross
Bell Green
COVENTRY CV1 9FH

A B Smith
23 Rectory Road
The Park
COVENTRY CV1 8XJ

16.3 Creating an envelope paper size

If your printer is capable of loading envelopes, then you can set up a special envelope paper size. If your printer will not take envelopes, then use labels instead.

1 Follow the usual procedure for setting up a new paper size, ie select Page from the Layout menu, followed by Paper Size/Type to display the relevant menu.

2 Select Add and then Envelope to display the **Format: Edit Paper Definition** screen.

3 Select Paper Size followed by Envelope if your envelopes are the size listed, or Other to key in your own particular size.

4 Select Location to set Manual feed and set Prompt to Load to **Yes**, so that you can load each envelope when asked.

5 Select the envelope definition and Exit to the text.

16.4 Using envelopes

1 Clear the screen, if necessary, and check that the Envelope definition is in your initial codes.

2 Set a left margin of about a third of the width of the envelope, and a top margin of 0", if you are going to load the envelope yourself [all printers except laser].

3 Key in the name and address for a single envelope or set up the fields for merging from a data file.

4 Print or merge, trying out the format on plain paper.

Activity 3

1 Set up an envelope size 6.75" x 4.5"

2 Load the file **LABEL.TMP**

3 Choose the envelope paper size, set a left margin of 2.5", a top margin of 0 and save as **ENVELOPE.TMP**

4 Merge it with the file **CUSTOMER.DAT** on paper, then on envelopes, if you have some

Further uses

1 Multiple tickets

2 Badges

Problem solving

- *The message 'Error: Labels will not fit on paper size' is displayed when you are defining your new label paper size.*

  You have defined a number of labels which will not fit on the paper size you have chosen. Check the paper size and the number of labels you have set and try again.

- *When you preview your labels, they are on separate pages.*

  You did not put the label page definition in the Initial Codes of your primary file. Use **Document** from the **Layout** menu, followed by **Initial Codes**. Then select **Page** from the **Layout** menu and select the label page size. Save the file, clear the screen and merge again.

- *You cannot load envelopes into your pinter, or they get stuck round the roller.*

  This is quite a common problem, which may not have a direct solution. Some printers will not reliably load envelopes. Your best strategy is to use labels, which can then be stuck onto the envelopes.

Unit 17

Reports

Overview Reports look most professional when they have sections numbered in a 'hierarchical' way, eg 1.1, 1.2, 1.2.1 or 1 a), 1 b), etc. Outlining in WordPerfect allows you to carry out this numbering automatically, using any numbering scheme you specify.

Existing skills

- Checking spelling
- Inserting the date automatically - Unit 6
- Changing fonts - Unit 11

New skills

- Using horizontal and vertical ruling lines
- Creating and using outlines

Important Horizontal and vertical ruling lines are used to give emphasis to text used in headings. Horizontal lines usually start at a margin and are placed directly above or below text, as in the examples below.

Two lines between margins

Lines as long as the text

One line below

Vertical lines are most commonly put in margins to show revisions, or as column markers.

17.1 Adding horizontal and vertical ruling lines

1 Select **Line** from the **Graphics** menu, followed by **Create Horizontal** or **Create Vertical** to display the relevant menu.

```
Graphics: Vertical Line
  1 - Horizontal Position           Full
  2 - Vertical Position             Baseline
  3 - Length of Line
  4 - Width of Line                 0.013"
  5 - Grey Shading (% of black)     100%
```

2 Select in turn each feature of the line you want to set, using the table for reference and Exit to the text.

MENU OPTION	EFFECT OF CHOICE ON LINES	
	HORIZONTAL LINES	VERTICAL LINES
1 – H	Start at margin, or at set position	Position at either margin, or set position
2 – V	Baseline of text, or set from top margin	Top, bottom, centre or set position
3 – L	Set length from start of line, unless set by default by choices of H and V	
4 – W	Set the width of the line; 0.02" is quite thick, 0.005" gives a fine line	
5 – G	Set the blackness of the line	

17.2 Editing ruling lines

1 Reveal codes, so that you can look for the code that defines a line you want to edit. They consist of all the choices made about the line.

```
[Hline:Full,Baseline,3.83",0.013",100%]
```

2 Move your cursor to just after the code for the line you want to edit.

3 Select **Lines** from the **Graphics** menu and then **Edit Horizontal** or **Edit Vertical**.

4 Make any changes you want through this menu, and Exit to the text.

Activity 1

1 Clear the screen, if necessary
2 Select A4 paper size, if necessary, with 1" margins all round
3 Enter the title **Report**, right justified, emboldened and in Extra large size
4 Create two horizontal lines with the following specifications

OPTION	NO	SETTING
Vertical Position	1 2	.9" from the top of the page; 1.4" from the top of the page
Horizontal Position	Both	Across the whole page, i.e. 1" from left margin, 7.27" long.
Width	1 2	0.08" 0.01"

5 Preview to check the display. Make any changes you need, including moving the second line slightly to take account of the exact size of text of your printer
6 Save the heading as file **UNIT17-1** and print the heading
7 Check your output and make any changes you think necessary

17.3 Creating an outline

1 Move the cursor to the place in your file where outlining is to begin.

2 Select **Outline** from the **Tools** menu, followed by **On**. The word *Outline* will be displayed at the bottom of the screen.

3 Press **Return** to generate the first level number - **I.** - and type a heading for this first section, followed by **Return**.

4 The next number - **II.** - will be generated. Key in the appropriate heading.

5 Press Tab as soon as a new number is generated to move to the next level number - **A.** - or Shift Tab to go back to the previous level.

```
I.  First heading
II. Second heading
[Tab]   A. First sub-heading
        B. Second sub-heading [Shift Tab]
III. Third heading
[Tab]   A. First sub-heading
[Tab]      1. First sub-section
           2. Second sub-section
```

17.4 Specifying outline numbering style

1 With your cursor at the beginning of the file, select **Define** from the **Tools** menu to display the **Paragraph Number Definition** screen.
This screen can also be used for automatic numbering of paragraphs not in outlines.

2 Choose the style of numbering you prefer, as displayed on screen, or choose option 6 and key in your own, eg numbers alone.

3 Exit to the text.

```
2 - Paragraph
3 - Outline
4 - Legal (1.1.1)
5 - Bullets
6 - User-defined
```

17.5 Numbering existing text

1 Choose the numbering style you want.

2 Move the cursor to the text, immediately before the items which are to be numbered.

3 Select **Outline** from the **Tools** menu, followed by **On**.

4 Move the cursor to each item in turn and press **Return** to generate a number. Insert any spaces you want after the number. Select **Outline** from the **Tools** menu, followed by **Off** to switch off outlining.

Activity 2

1 If you have already completed Unit 12, and so have file AGENDA.TMP stored on disk, then load it and delete the numbers and the blank lines between items
or
Key in the agenda below, omitting the item numbers
2 Specify legal numbering for outlines
3 Turn on Outline mode and generate numbers for each item, with 2 spaces after it
4 Save and print one copy

```
                    A G E N D A
1  Apologies
2  Minutes of last meeting
3  Matters arising
4
5
6
7
8
9  Any other business
10 Date and time of next meeting
```

Activity 3

1. Load the file **UNIT17-1**, if it is not already on screen
2. Set page size to A4, if necessary
3. Choose legal numbering and set tabs at 0.5" intervals
4. Key in the report template shown below, using outlining to produce the numbering, and following the display given
5. When blank lines are required, use Backspace to delete the number immediately it is generated
6. Proofread on screen and spell check. This is particularly important for files which are to be used as templates for other documents
7. Turn off outlining before the signature, so that it is not numbered
8. Print out a copy for reference and save to disk as file **REPORT.TMP**

Report

To: **Date:**

1 **Subject:**

2 **Terms of Reference**

2.1
2.2
2.3

3 **Procedure**
3.1
3.2
3.3

4 **Findings**
4.1

5 **Conclusions**
5.1
5.2

6 **Recommendations**
6.1
6.2

Signature:
Designation:

Activity 4

1 If you have already completed Unit 14 and have **UNIT14-1** on disk, then retrieve it
2 Choose legal numbering
3 Move through the minutes, removing the typed numbering and generating automatic numbers for each item
4 Preview, check the display and print, if desired

10 **Any other business**

10.1 **Company Cars** Nat Singh asked if the Chairman knew of any change in policy on company cars. The Chairman replied that he had heard various rumours circulating but these were without foundation and there was no change in policy.

10.2 **Redundancies** Carol Breedon asked if there was any truth in the rumour regarding redundancies in the firm as a whole. The Chairman said that some cut backs would be necessary but that it was hoped to achieve these by natural wastage; no redundancies were planned at this time.

Activity 5

1 Retrieve the report template you prepared in Activity 3, saved on disk as **REPORT.TMP**, if it is not already on screen
2 Use the template to produce the report which is given below and on the next page
3 Generate the date automatically
4 Use Backspace delete to remove any unwanted numbering in blank lines
5 Check the display, save and print

Report

To: The Managing Director **Date:** today's date

1 **Subject: FLEXITIME**

2 **Terms of Reference**

2.1 At your request, I undertook to ascertain whether the office staff would be prepared to change over to flexible working hours.

2.2 I also undertook to produce a report within four weeks.

3 **Procedure**

3.1 I initially circulated a questionnaire.

3.2 I followed this up with personal interviews, in order to establish the main body of opinion.

3.3 I made preliminary investigations into the equipment needed to run the scheme.

4 **Findings**

4.1 The results of the questionnaire and interviews were in favour of flexitime.

4.2 There were only two or three members of senior staff who would not welcome the change.

4.3 Most staff appreciated that they would be able to accommodate personal arrangements more easily and to accrue time sufficient to allow for the occasional long week-end.

5 **Conclusions**

5.1 I concluded that the change could be effected without opposition and with the minimum disruption of office procedures.

5.2 The advantages would include reducing the need for overtime and enabling staff to travel outside peak commuter hours.

5.3 The system should also eliminate bad timekeeping.

6 **Recommendations**

6.1 I recommend that the Company changes over to flexitime for office staff from the beginning of April.

6.2 An April start would allow sufficient time for the installation of a special time recorder and the issue of individual keys to all staff in the system.

Signature: Marie Bossicco
Designation: Personal Assistant

Further uses

1 Vertical ruling lines between columns (*see* Unit 21)

2 Composing reports at the keyboard

3 Structuring any piece of work

Problem solving

- *One or both of your horizontal lines does not begin at the left margin and end at the right margin.*

  You set the horizontal position incorrectly. Reveal codes, then move the cursor to the right of the appropriate line code and edit, using **Graphics Line Edit Horizontal**.

- *Your horizontal lines are the same width, rather than thick above the text and thin below it.*

  You set an incorrect line width for one of them. Reveal codes, then move the cursor to highlight the appropriate line code and edit it.

- *Your horizontal lines are the wrong way round, rather than thick above the text and thin below it.*

  You set an incorrect width for both lines. Reveal codes, then move the cursor to highlight each line code in turn and edit them, using **Graphics Line Edit Horizontal**.

- *Your lines are incorrect, but you cannot change their features.*

  Reveal codes and move the cursor to the code immediately on the right of the appropriate code to edit it, using **Graphics Line Edit Horizontal**.

- *The body of your report is overwritten by the second ruling line of the heading.*

  Your printer spacing leaves very little room above text. Insert a blank line before the first line of the report to leave a little more space for the ruling line.

- *You have numbering in your outline on lines which are supposed to be blank.*

  You did not backspace delete the number as it was generated. Move your cursor and delete it now. Alternatively, you can reveal codes and delete the code **[Par Num:Auto]** from the appropriate line.

Unit 18

Legal documents

Overview

Legal work should not be punctuated, as the language used should be sufficiently clear without the aid of such means of expression. The final copy of any legal document should be error free, so as to reduce the possibility of misinterpretation or fraud.

The clauses in legal documents are similar for each particular document, eg Conveyance, Agreement, Will, Trust Deed, and lend themselves to a WP library.

Existing skills

- Checking spelling - Unit 2
- Numbering paragraphs - Unit 5
- Setting tabs - Unit 7
- Changing fonts - Unit 11
- Splitting pages - Unit 14

New skills

- Double spacing

Important For legal work, you should spell check initially and then proofread carefully against your original.

18.1 Setting initial base font

1 Select **Document** from the **Layout** menu, followed by **Initial Base Font**.

2 Highlight the font your require and **Select** it. Exit to the text.

3 All text in your document will be in the new font.

Activity 1

1 Clear the screen, if necessary, select the base font Roman PS or Times Roman 9 point and key in the following deed of trust

2 Spell check, proof read carefully and save on disk as **UNIT18-1**

DECLARATION OF THE TRUSTS OF THE EMMA SHAW MEMORIAL TRUST

THIS DECLARATION OF TRUST made on .... 19.. by Alan Holmes of 12 Kuster Road West Bridgford Nottingham and Marjory Elliott of 5 Wilmore Drive West Bridgford Nottingham and the Reverend Austen Williams of The Vicarage Church Road West Bridgford Nottingham (referred to herein as "the Trustees" which expression shall include the trustees for the time being of this deed)

WITNESSES as follows:

1 There is established by this deed a charitable trust ("the Trust") to be known as The Emma Shaw Memorial Trust

2 The objects of the Trust shall be to distribute and pay all money and other assets of the Trust (whether capital or income) to (whether capital or income) and for such charitable purposes and in such manner and in such proportions as the Trustees in their absolute discretion shall think fit AND in particular (though without prejudice to the generality of the foregoing) to and for the maintenance and support of persons connected with the Church of England in the Parish of St Peter's at West Bridgford who are engaged in a course of Christian study or who are training for the Ministry of the Church of England

3 The initial money and assets of the Trust are as stated in the Schedule to this deed AND the Trustees may collect and receive money for the purposes of the Trust by donation or in such other lawful manner as they shall think fit

4 The receipt of any person who shall be an object of or who shall be acting in any responsible capacity in respect of any charitable purpose shall be a good discharge to the Trustees for any payment or transfer of assets made for the relevant purpose

5 The Trustees may for such period as is permitted by law in their absolute discretion accumulate all or any of the income of the Trust by investing it and shall hold such accumulations as an addition to the capital of the Trust AND the Trustees shall have power to invest any money for the time being not required for the purposes of the Trust in any investment authorised for the investment of trust money or by placing it on deposit at any bank or building society in Great Britain

6 THE power of appointing new or additional trustees of the Trust shall be vested in the Vicar for the time being of the Parish of St Peter's aforesaid

7 THE expression "charitable purposes" means purposes which are exclusively charitable according to the law for the time being of England and Wales

8 THE Trustees shall distribute the whole of the money and other assets held by them for the purposes of the Trust in accordance with clause 2 hereof on or before the expiration of one hundred years from the date hereof

9 IN WITNESS whereof the parties hereto have hereunto set their hands the day and year first before written

THE SCHEDULE

Three hundred and fifty thousand pounds invested in a Capital Reserve Account with the Cooperative Bank plc
Two hundred and five thousand pounds invested in a Gold Account with the Alliance and Leicester Building Society
Twenty five thousand pounds invested in a ninety day account with the Halifax Building Society
One thousand shares in British Telecom
Two thousand shares in British Gas

SIGNED AS A DEED by the said Alan Holmes)
in the presence of)

SIGNED AS A DEED by the said Marjory Elliott)
in the presence of)

SIGNED AS A DEED by the said Austen Williams)
in the presence of)

18.2 Setting double spacing

1 Move the cursor to the place in the text where double spacing is to begin.

2 Select **Line** from the **Layout** menu, followed by **Line Spacing** and key in **2** for double line spacing.

3 Exit to the text.

Activity 2

1 Retrieve the file **UNIT18-1**, if it is not already on screen
2 Delete the blank lines between paragraphs and set double spacing after the heading. Set single spacing again after the heading 'The Schedule'
3 Preview to check display, insert a page break in a suitable place, save and print

DECLARATION OF THE TRUSTS OF THE EMMA SHAW MEMORIAL TRUST

THIS DECLARATION OF TRUST made on . . . . 19.. by Alan Holmes of 12 Kuster Road West Bridgford Nottingham and Marjory Elliott of 5 Wilmore Drive West Bridgford Nottingham and the Reverend Austen Williams of The Vicarage Church Road West Bridgford Nottingham (referred to herein as "the Trustees" which expression shall include the trustees for the time being of this deed)
WITNESSES as follows:

1 There is established by this deed a charitable trust ("the Trust") to be known as The Emma Shaw Memorial Trust

2 The objects of the Trust shall be to distribute and pay all money and other assets of the Trust (whether capital or income) to (whether capital or income) and for such charitable purposes and in such manner and in such proportions as the Trustees in their absolute discretion shall think fit AND in particular (though without prejudice to the generality of the foregoing) to and for the maintenance and support of persons connected with the Church of England in the Parish of St Peter's at West Bridgford who are engaged in a course of Christian study or who are training for the Ministry of the Church of England

3 The initial money and assets of the Trust are as stated in the Schedule to this deed AND the Trustees may collect and receive money for the purposes of the Trust by donation or in such other lawful manner as they shall think fit

4 The receipt of any person who shall be an object of or who shall be acting in any responsible capacity in respect of any charitable purpose shall be a good discharge to the Trustees for any payment or transfer of assets made for the relevant purpose

5 The Trustees may for such period as is permitted by law in their absolute discretion accumulate all or any of the income of the Trust by investing it and shall hold such accumulations as an addition to the capital of the Trust AND the Trustees shall have power to invest any money for the time being not required for the purposes of the Trust in any investment authorised for the investment of trust money or by placing it on deposit at any bank or building society in Great Britain

6 THE power of appointing new or additional trustees of the Trust shall be vested in the Vicar for the time being of the Parish of St Peter's aforesaid

7 THE expression "charitable purposes" means purposes which are exclusively charitable according to the law for the time being of England and Wales

8 THE Trustees shall distribute the whole of the money and other assets held by them for the purposes of the Trust in accordance with clause 2 hereof on or before the expiration of one hundred years from the date hereof

9 IN WITNESS whereof the parties hereto have hereunto set their hands the day and year first before written

THE SCHEDULE

Three hundred and fifty thousand pounds invested in a Capital Reserve Account with the Cooperative Bank plc
Two hundred and five thousand pounds invested in a Gold Account with the Alliance and Leicester Building Society
Twenty five thousand pounds invested in a ninety day account with the Halifax Building Society
One thousand shares in British Telecom
Two thousand shares in British Gas

SIGNED AS A DEED by the said)
Alan Holmes in the presence)
of)

SIGNED AS A DEED by the said)
Marjory Elliott in the)
presence of)

SIGNED AS A DEED by the said)
Austen Williams in the)
presence of)

Further uses

1 Variable line spacing is used when designing forms

2 Double or treble line spacing is used in drafts, literary work, legal documents or similar work

Problem solving

- *Your final document is not in double line spacing.*

  Your cursor was not at the beginning of the file when you selected double spacing. Move the cursor to the beginning and select it again. Preview to check the display.

- *Your brackets are not aligned before the signatures.*

  You did not use Tab to align them. Set up a tab stop at the appropriate place, if one does not already exist, and insert tabs before the brackets.

Unit 19

Literary work

Overview

Literary documents have a set of standard rules. Footnotes are used for explanation and headers and footers for chapters and the book title. Spelling is particularly important to give a good impression, and authors often use a Thesaurus to look up alternative words; to avoid using the same word several times, which is considered bad style.

Existing skills

- Checking spelling - Unit 2
- Indented paras - Unit 5
- Splitting pages - Unit 14
- Using headers and footers - Unit 14

New skills

- Using footnotes
- Using a Thesaurus

Important Footnotes are references or additional items of explanation inserted at the bottom of the appropriate page, with a small number, letter or character in the text for reference.

Footnotes are not displayed on the editing screen. They can be seen only in Preview.

> Footnotes are references or additional items of explanation inserted at the bottom of the appropriate page, with a small number, letter or character in the text for reference.
> Footnotes[1] are references or additional items of explanation inserted at the bottom of the appropriate page, with a small number, letter or character in the text for reference.
> ------
> [1] This is the footnote

19.1 Creating a footnote

1 Position your cursor immediately after the word to which the footnote is to refer.

2 Select **Footnote** from the **Layout** menu, followed by **Create**.

3 An editing screen, with the word **Footnote** at the bottom, will be displayed.

4 If this is the first footnote, then the number **1** will be displayed at the cursor position - this is its default number.

5 Type in the explanation and then Exit to the text.

6 Preview to see the footnote.

7 Carry out the same procedure for any further footnotes.

19.2 Setting the numbering method

1 Select **Footnote** from the **Layout** menu, followed by **Options** to display the **Footnote Options** screen.

2 Select **Footnote Numbering Method** and choose the numbering system you want, ie **N**umbers, **L**etters or **C**haracters.

3 If you choose characters, you wil also have to choose the character you want, eg *.

4 Exit to the text.

Important You can make a number of other choices through this options menu, including the maximum space on the page allocated to footnotes, where the footnotes are placed, the text style used and the presence of a line separating them from the text.

Activity 1

1 Clear the screen, if necessary
2 Key in the Authors' Word Processing Rules, using the display given on page 119
3 Set up the footnotes shown on the sheet
4 Preview to check the display, save as **UNIT19-1** and print

Word Processing for Authors

Word processing is an ideal author's tool, as alterations and redrafts are made easily and quickly. Literary work covers reports, articles, short stories, books or theses. There are a few rules to remember:

Stationery Usually one side of A4 is used.

Line Spacing Reports are usually single line spaced but manuscripts for books and stories should be double line spaced.

Margins Margins should not be less than 25 mm each side but if a binding margin is required the left margin should be 38 mm and the right 13 mm to 25 mm.[1] The top and bottom margins should be equal at 25 mm[2] except for chapter headings.

Pagination Use automatic pagination for numbering the pages. Ensure that single lines are not separated from the main text, leaving widows and orphans. Check that lists of items are not separated from one another. Use the 'widow/orphan protection' function to avoid mistakes.

Chapter heading The first page of a chapter is often in the form of a 'dropped head' which is when the chapter number is printed 51 mm to 76 mm from the top edge of the paper.

Layout The layout should be consistent throughout the work.

Footnotes Footnotes are usually printed at the foot of the page to which they refer. A number or symbol, such as asterisk, is shown in the text closed up to the referenced word. The footnote commences with the symbol and, after one space, the reference is given.

Spelling Check Make full use of the spelling check not only for mis-spelt words but also to pick up typos.

Thesaurus The Thesaurus is an invaluable tool in literary work.

Headers and Footers Headers and footers are useful in literary work. The header might be the title of the work and a footer, in addition to the page numbers, could give the author's name.

----

[1] If both sides of the paper are used, and the margins are unequal, then margins may be reversed on the continuation sheets.

[2] 1" in imperial measure.

19.3 Using the Thesaurus

A Thesaurus is a special sort of dictionary which gives alternative words with the same or a similar meaning. WordPerfect has a disk-based version which can be used when a word you have chosen does not seem to fit well, or has been used already in the same sentence or paragraph.

1 Position the cursor on the word you wish to look up in the Thesaurus.

2 Select **Thesaurus** from the **Tools** menu to display a screen which shows all the possible alternatives, listed in alphabetical groups for each meaning of the word .

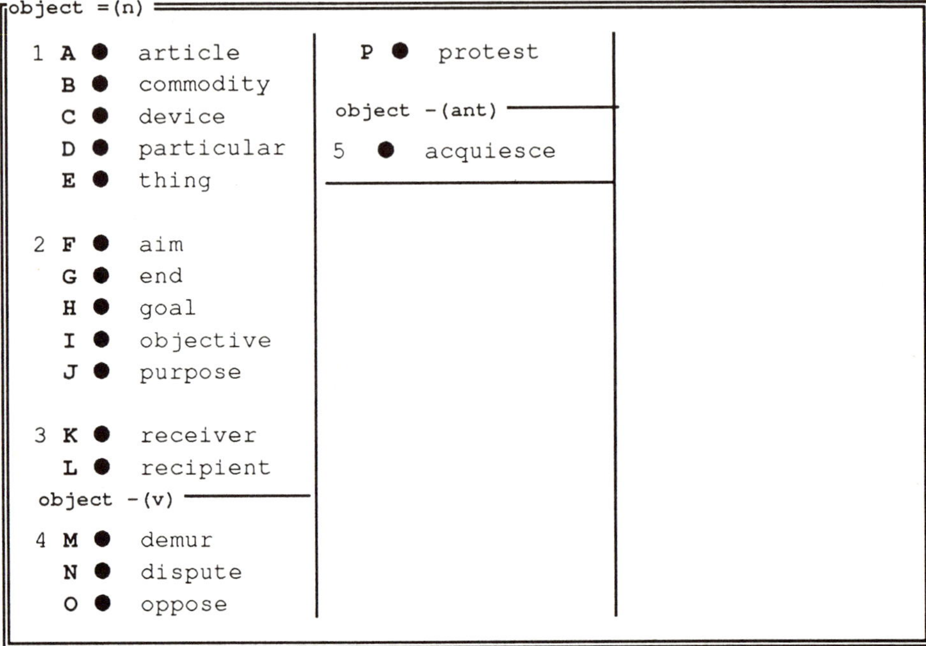

object =(n)
1 A ● article
B ● commodity
C ● device
D ● particular
E ● thing
2 F ● aim
G ● end
H ● goal
I ● objective
J ● purpose
3 K ● receiver
L ● recipient
object -(v)
4 M ● demur
N ● dispute
O ● oppose
P ● protest
object -(ant)
5 ● acquiesce

3 Press **1** to replace the word, followed with the letter of the word you want.

4 The word will be replaced in your text.

Activity 2

1 Clear the screen, if necessary

2 If you have completed Unit 20 and so have **UNIT18-1** saved on disk, retrieve it and find the word 'objects'

or

Key in the word 'objects'

3 Use the Thesaurus to choose an alternative for 'objects' which has the same meaning as in a legal document

Activity 3

1 Clear the screen and key in the following start of a romantic novel
2 Use the chapter number as a header and your own name as a footer
3 Use the spelling checker for corrections and then the Thesaurus to replace 'muttered' and 'worrying' for similar words
4 Remember that you will have to check that your choice of word fits, eg choosing 'laboured' to replace 'worked', rather than 'labour', which would not fit the sentence
5 Add the footnote which gives the Latin name of the plant
6 Save as **UNIT19-1** and print

CHAPTER I

THE QUARREL

Tina worked furiously in the garden ostensibly weeding but, in her present state of mind, plants also flew in profusion. She didn't even notice when she uprooted her favourite Meadow Rue[a]. She was desperately hoping the telephone would ring. She and her boy friend, Rick, had quarrelled badly last night and she was now full of regrets and worrying over what they had said.

It was such a silly row and started over the meal. She had gone to a great deal of trouble to cook a special meal for their anniversary; it was one month since they had met. She had served melon and avocado cocktail followed by lemon chicken and she thought that her Charlotte Russe for dessert was a masterpiece. Rick had hardly eaten a thing and muttered something about a big lunch. She thought he'd spent too long at the pub before turning up and so, of course, her temper had risen. Before she realised it, they were both arguing and she said some things that she now regretted. Rick flung out of the flat and left her in tears amongst the debris of the meal.

She thought about the day that they had met. It was late on a Friday evening and she had gone down to her local supermarket to stock up for the week-end. She was just about to select a small chicken, when it was wrenched, almost from her hand, and she turned startled to find a tall, blonde and very handsome man had picked it up. As he met her indignant gaze, he realised what he had done and apologised profusely. He said 'May I buy you a drink to make amends for my bad manners?' Although Tina did not usually make casual dates, she found his steel grey eyes quite magnetic and found herself agreeing. Things had moved rapidly on from there.

----

[a] Thalictrum aquilegifolium

Further uses

1 Explanatory notes in business documents

2 Choosing appropriate language for any composition work

Problem solving

- *There is no line separating the footnotes from the text.*

  This option is not set. Select **Footnote** from the **Layout** menu, followed by **Options**. Then select **7** or **L**ine and select a **2**-inch or **M**argin to produce a Margin line.

- *A word you want to look up gives no alternatives.*

  The word is not in the Thesaurus, so no alternatives are available. A disk based Thesaurus contains only a limited number of the most commonly used words, unlike the appropriate reference book.

- *The word you have chosen as an alternative from the Thesaurus does not seem to fit the sentence.*

  You have chosen from the wrong list of alternatives for a word which has several different meanings. Change back to the original word, then use the Thesaurus again and choose from another list.

- *The word you have chosen as an alternative from the Thesaurus seems to change the meaning of the sentence.*

  You may have chosen the antonym, which is the exact opposite in meaning for a word. It is listed at the end under the heading **-(ant)**. Delete the word, key in the original word and choose again.

Unit 20

Scientific work

Overview When doing scientific work, you will need to use the special facilities in WordPerfect for producing equations.

Existing skills

- Enhancing text - Unit 3

New skills

- Using subscript and superscript
- Creating equations

Important The facilities provided in WordPerfect allow you to enter, display and edit an equation which forms an integral part of a document. They do not allow you to make any calculations based on those equations. The way in which equations work is exactly the same in both versions, although the menu choices vary very slightly and you have a little more control over alignment in WordPerfect for Windows.

20.1 Using superscript

Superscript gives **raised** characters which should be half the size of normal text in scientific/mathematical work, eg $\mathbf{x}^2$.

1. Select the text to be enhanced with the mouse, or move your cursor to the first letter of the text, select **Block** from the **Edit** menu and use the cursor to highlight.
2. Select **Superscript** from the **Font** menu. If printing shows that the superscript is not half size, then also select **Fine** from the **Font** menu.
3. The text will now be shown in colour or highlighting on your screen, depending on your display.

20.2 Using subscript

Subscript gives **lowered** characters which should be half the size of normal text in scientific/mathematical work, eg $\mathbf{X}_0$.

1. Select the text to be enhanced with the mouse, or move your cursor to the first letter of the text, select **Block** from the **Edit** menu and use the cursor to highlight.
2. Select **Superscript** from the **Font** menu. If printing shows that the superscript is not half size, then also select **Fine** from the **Font** menu.
3. The text will now be shown in colour or highlighting on your screen, depending on your display.

Activity 1

1. Clear the screen, if necessary
2. Key in the following chemical explanation, following the display given
3. Check, preview, save as **UNIT20-1** and print

Neutralising values

The equation for the reaction of calcium hydroxide (slaked lime) with hydrochloric acid is:

$Ca(OH)_2(s)$ + 2HCl(aq) ===> $CaCl_2(aq)$ +$H_2O(l)$

1 mol of calcium oxide neutralises the same amount of acid as 1 mol of calcium hydroxide.
The molar mass of calcium oxide = 56 g/mol
The molar mass of calcium hydroxide = 74 g/mol

20.3 Creating an equation

1 Select **Equation** from the **Graphics** menu, followed by **Create** to display the **Definition: Equation** screen.

2 Select **Edit** to display the Equation Editor screen.

3 Key in your equation, using the usual arithmetical operators, ie plus, minus, multiply *, divide /, together with the commands listed at the right hand side of the screen (press **F5** to highlight them).

4 Press key **F9** to see your equation in the box.

5 Exit to your text. You can see the equation only in preview.

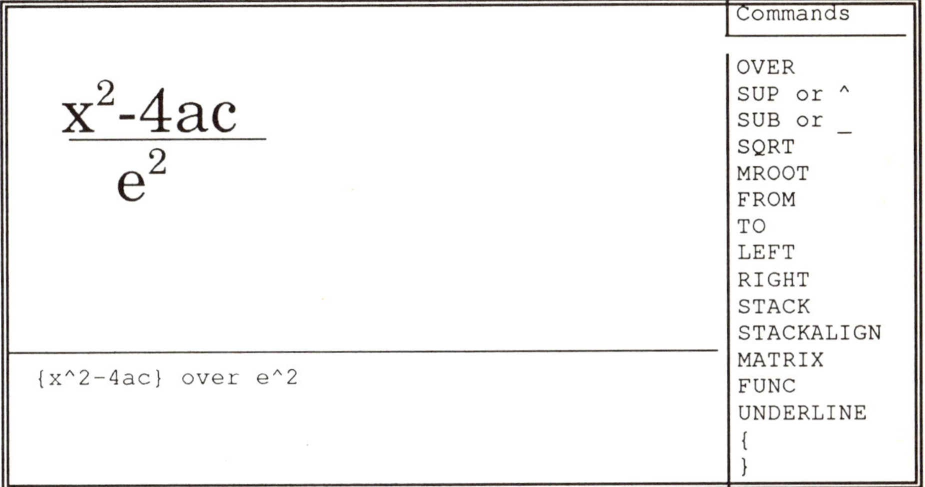

Activity 2

1 Retrieve the file **UNIT20-1**, if it is not already on screen
2 Add the equation to the file, as shown below
3 Preview, save and print

Neutralising values
The equation for the reaction of calcium hydroxide (slaked lime) with hydrochloric acid is:

$Ca(OH)_2(s)$ + 2HCl(aq) ===> $CaCl_2(aq)$ +$H_2O(l)$

1 mol of calcium oxide neutralises the same amount of acid as 1 mol of calcium hydroxide.
The molar mass of calcium oxide = 56 g/mol
The molar mass of calcium hydroxide = 74 g/mol
so 100g of calcium hydroxide will neutralise the same amount of acid as

$\frac{100}{74} \times 56g = 75.7g$ of calcium oxide

Further uses

1 Educational work

2 Mathematical work

Problem solving

- *Your subscripted letters are not highlighted on a monochrome screen.*

  You chose a colour for subscript which does not show up on monochrome. Use **File Setup Display Colours** to set a stronger colour.

- *Your subscripted text is not shown in preview or when printed.*

  Reveal codes and check that the **[SUBSCPT**] and **[subscpt]** codes are at each side of the letter to be subscripted. If not, delete them, highlight the letter and select subscript again.

- *You have tried the equation shown on the sample screen and the line is under only 4ac, instead of* x^2*-4ac.*

  You missed out the brackets round x^2-4ac when entering the equation. Edit the definition to include the brackets.

Unit 21

Newsletters

Overview With a suitable printer, you can produce a newsletter of a quality good enough for internal circulation. If you want complicated display, or unusual fonts, then you should use only the Windows version of WordPerfect, or a DTP package.

Existing skills

- Changing text size - Unit 4
- Revealing codes - Unit 5
- Using styles - Unit 13
- Ruling lines - Unit 17

New skills

- Using multiple columns
- Importing graphics

Important There are 2 types of column available in WordPerfect, Newspaper and Parallel. Newspaper columns allow text to flow from the bottom of one column to the top of the next, as in a newspaper. Parallel columns are better produced using a multi-line table (*see* Unit 9).

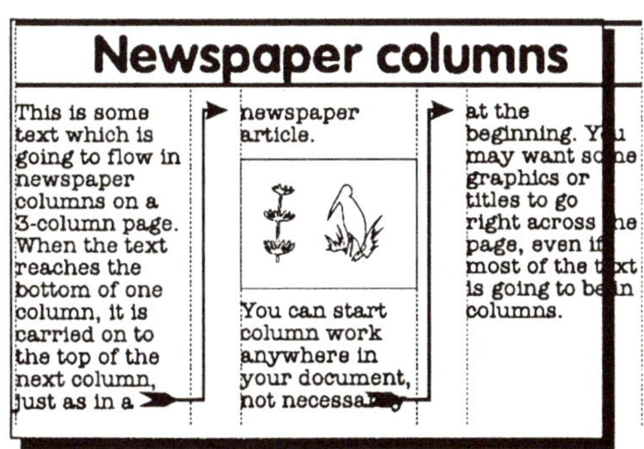

Newspaper columns
This is some text which is going to flow in newspaper columns on a 3-column page. When the text reaches the bottom of one column, it is carried on to the top of the next column, just as in a
newspaper article.
You can start column work anywhere in your document, not
at the beginning.
may want
graphics or titles to go right across
page, even
most of the
is going to
columns.

21.1 Setting up multiple columns

Using WordPerfect you can have up to 24 columns, but you will rarely want more than 3 or 4, unless you are using very small text. Before you can use multiple columns, you have to define them.

1 Select **Columns** from the **Layout** menu, followed by **Define** to display the **Text Column Definition** menu.

```
Text Column Definition

1 - Type                                 Newspaper
2 - Number of Columns                    2
3 - Distance Between Columns
4 - Margins

Column    Left     Right     Column    Left     Right
 1:       1"       3.88"     13:
 2:       4.38"    7.27"     14:
```

2 If Type is not already set to **Newspaper**, select **1** or **T**ype and then **1** or **N**ewpaper from the menu.

3 Choose the number of columns you require. Margin measurements for each column will be displayed, which fill your page and leave a gutter of 0.5".

4 When all selections have been made, Exit to the text.

5 A menu will be displayed at the bottom of the screen. Select **1** or **O**n to switch on columns if you want to start using columns at the current cursor position, otherwise select **D**efine.

Activity 1

1 Clear the screen, if necessary
2 Define 4 Newspaper columns with .25" between each
3 Reveal codes and check that you have the code given below in your file
4 Save the file as **UNIT21-1**

```
[Col Def:Newspaper;4;1",2.38";2.63",4.01";4.26",5.64";5.89",7.27"]
```

21.2 Using multiple columns

1. Move the cursor to the point where multiple columns are to begin.
2. Select **Columns** from the **Layout** menu, followed by **On**.
3. A `[Col On]` code will be inserted in your file.
4. When columns are to end, follow the same procedure, selecting **Off**.

21.3 Displaying columns

You can choose whether or not columns are displayed on the screen while you are editing. In general, it is best to do so, as this makes it easier to see what you are doing, but if you have a large file, this display mode may be slow. You can, in any case, see columns display in Preview.

1. Select **Setup** from the **File** menu, followed by **Display** and **Edit-Screen Options**.
2. Check that the selection for **S**ide-by-side Columns Display is **Yes**. If the selection is **No**, change to **Yes**.
3. Exit to the text.

Activity 2

1. Load up the file **UNIT21-1**, if it is not already on screen. Check that you are displaying Side-by-side columns
2. If you have completed Unit 14, retrieve the minutes saved as **UNIT14-1** into this file. Alternatively, you can use the file **UNIT18-1**, the trust deed saved in Unit 18
3. Move the cursor to the first line after the heading and switch on columns. The top of your page should look like the sample shown below, although the columns may split differently
4. Save, preview and print

Minutes of a meeting of Midlands Sales Staff at Soar House, New Road, Leicester, on Wednesday, 12 March 19.., at 1000 hours.

Present

Michael Schaal (Chairman)
Chris Booth
Carol Breedon
Kelly Jay
Mike Oates
Judy Prior
Tina Salami
Anne Simpson
Nat Singh
Paul Ure
Jo Van Gyseghem
Brad West
Tam Wyatt
Mel Winters (Secretary)

subject after the meeting.

4 **Business review**

The Chairman presented charts and graphs showing the present position in the Midlands. The Company was 37% below target in the present financial year; the area 19% below. The reflection of the country's present economic position..

5 **Targets**

Tam Wyatt circulated copies of the February sales targets results. The Chairman congratulated Tina Salami on achieving top sales and said that she had become a valuable member there would be a promotion on the Golden bar range offeing a 10p money-back coupon on next purchase.

Sales promotional materials, samples and dump bins were provided for sales people to collect at the meeting

7 **Visits**

21.4 Setting options for graphics boxes

Graphics boxes are the method through which most graphics features are achieved in WordPerfect. If you have completed Unit 20, you will already have used Equation boxes. There are four other types of boxes, but they do not vary a great deal in use, so only Figure boxes are used here. Before any boxes can be created, a style has to be set for them.

1 Select **Figure** from the **Graphics** menu followed by **Options** to display the menu.

2 Select each item in the **Border Style** and **Border Space** options which you wish to change from the default settings given.

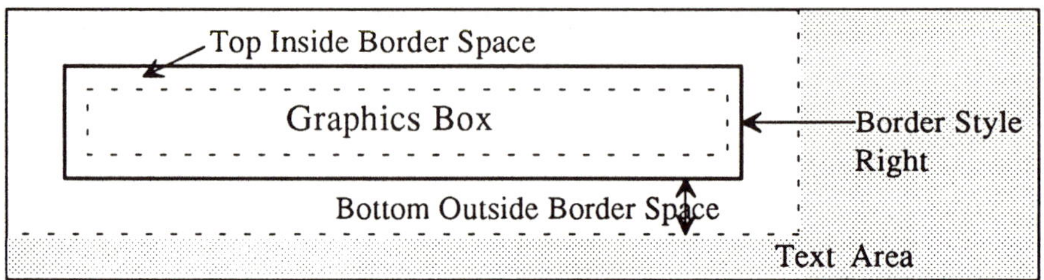

3 If you want a caption attached to the box, for example if it is to hold a diagram for a report, choose a position for it and set the style.

4 Exit to the text. A **[Fig Opt]** code will have been put into your file.

Activity 3

1 Load up the file **UNIT21-1**, if it is not already on screen

2 With the cursor at the beginning of the file, set up the following **G**raphics **F**igure **O**ptions

Border Style	**None**	no lines around the box
Outside Border Space	0.1"	on all 4 sides
Inside Border Space	0"	on all 4 sides

3 Exit to the text and check that you have a code in the file

4 Save the file for further use

21.5 Using graphics boxes for text

You can place text in a specified position on the page by putting it in a graphics box. This is a useful facility if you wish to display a title across more than one column, for example.

1 Move the cursor to the position in the text where the box is to appear.

2 Select **Figure** from the **Graphics** menu, followed by **Create**. The menu displayed has all the options needed to define any box contents. The options needed for text are explained below.

OPTION	EXPLANATION
3 - **C**aption	Optional attached title for box
4 - Anchor **T**ype	Box is set to move with text, a **character** or **paragraph**, or to be on a specified **page**
5 - **V**ertical Position	Measurement of distance of box from text or from the top of the page
6 - **H**orizontal Position	Position on page, or relative to margins
7 - **S**ize	Set width, height or both
8 - **W**rap Text Around Box	Sets whether text goes round box or over it.
9 - **E**dit	Allows entry of text with any special codes, such as alignment, font, appearance.

3 Set the options for the size and position you want. Use the **Edit** option to type in the text you require, setting any special codes you are going to use.

4 Exit to the text. A code, such as those shown in the example below, will be displayed on screen.

5 Preview to see how the boxes fit on the page.

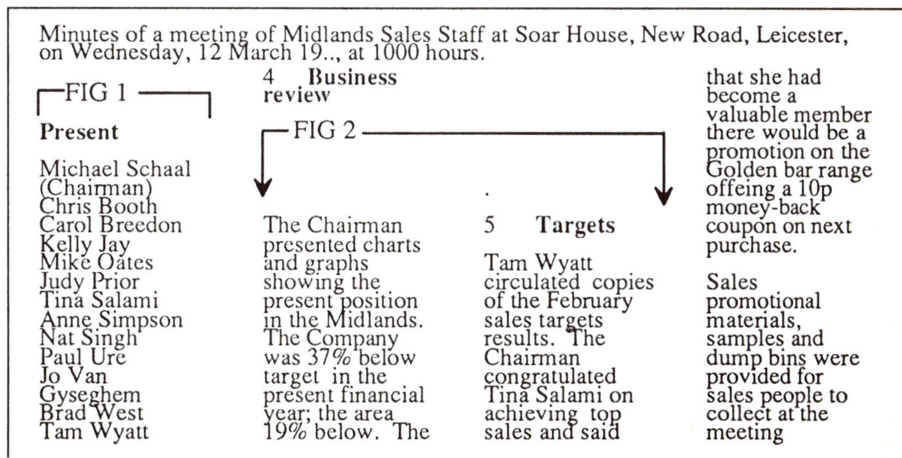

Minutes of a meeting of Midlands Sales Staff at Soar House, New Road, Leicester, on Wednesday, 12 March 19.., at 1000 hours.

FIG 1

Present

Michael Schaal (Chairman)
Chris Booth
Carol Breedon
Kelly Jay
Mike Oates
Judy Prior
Tina Salami
Anne Simpson
Nat Singh
Paul Ure
Jo Van Gyseghem
Brad West
Tam Wyatt

4 **Business review**

FIG 2

The Chairman presented charts and graphs showing the present position in the Midlands. The Company was 37% below target in the present financial year; the area 19% below. The

5 **Targets**

Tam Wyatt circulated copies of the February sales targets results. The Chairman congratulated Tina Salami on achieving top sales and said that she had become a valuable member there would be a promotion on the Golden bar range offeing a 10p money-back coupon on next purchase.

Sales promotional materials, samples and dump bins were provided for sales people to collect at the meeting

Activity 4

1 Load up the file **UNIT21-1**
2 Create a Graphics Figure with a Page anchor, a distance of 3" from the top of the page, across the first 2 columns [Horizontal position - **Column(s) 1-2, Full**] setting the size to 3" wide with automatic height
3 Enter the text **Column Title** at the Editing screen, setting codes to embolden, centre and make the text Extra Large
4 Exit to the text and preview to check that the box is in the correct position. It should have no border, because this was one of the options set in Activity 3
5 Save and print

Minutes of a meeting of Midlands Sales Staff at Soar House, New Road, Leicester, on Wednesday, 12 March 19.., at 1000 hours.

Present

Michael Schaal (Chairman)
Chris Booth
Carol Breedon
Kelly Jay
Mike Oates
Judy Prior
Tina Salami
Anne Simpson
Nat Singh
Paul Ure
Jo Van Gyseghem
Brad West
Tam Wyatt

Column Title

4 **Business review**

The Chairman presented charts and graphs showing the present position in the Midlands. The Company was 37% below target in the present financial year; the area 19% below. The

5 **Targets**

Tam Wyatt circulated copies of the February sales targets results. The Chairman congratulated Tina Salami on achieving top sales and said that she had become a valuable member

there would be a promotion on the Golden bar range offeing a 10p money-back coupon on next purchase.

Sales promotional materials, samples and dump bins were provided for sales people to collect at the meeting

7 **Visits**

21.6 Editing graphics boxes

If you are not happy with the graphics box you have created, you can delete it and start again or, more usefully, you can edit its setting to make any amendments you want. This is particularly useful if you merely want to move the box slightly, or to edit the text within it.

1 Reveal codes in your file and highlight the code **[Figure:n;;]** which defines the box.
2 Select **Figure** from the **Graphics** menu, followed by **Edit**. You will be asked to confirm the number of the Figure you want to edit.
3 The **Definition: Figure** menu will be displayed, with the current settings displayed also.
4 Make any amendments you want and Exit to the text.
5 Preview to check your settings are correct.
6 Re-edit to make any further changes needed and save.

Activity 5

1 Clear the screen, if necessary, and key in the text given below
2 Proofread on screen, spell check and save as file **UNIT21-2**

```
Most drawing programs are capable of the following: text
in several sizes, weights and styles; simple shapes, such
as rectangles, circles and arcs; lines of different
thicknesses at any angle and shading in various weights or
patterns.
The program may be a separate package or part of a more
comprehensive package, such as Desk Top Publishing.
There are a number of ways in which drawing packages can
be used, producing simple diagrams; positioning large text
on a page and for simple drawings.
Pie chart
A single pie chart can be used to present only one set of
figures. Each figure is shown as a percentage of the total
of all the figures, with the angle of each pie slice
representing the percentage. It is only suitable for
situations when the total is significant; in any other
situation, a pie chart will be inappropriate and will give
false information.
Bar chart
A bar chart uses the length of bars of equal width to
represent one set of numerical values. It enables
comparison between the values in the set, merely by
looking at the lengths.
Multiple bar chart
If you have more than one set of figures, and comparisons
are to be made between sets, as well as between figures in
the same set, then multiple bar charts are used. The bars
can be stacked, ie the second set on top of the first set,
in which case the total of the two sets can also be
compared. Alternatively, the bars can be next to each
other, in which case shading is used to pick out each set
of figures.
Line graph
If you are mainly interested in the change in one or more
set of figures, then a line graph may be suitable, where
points are plotted and joined with lines, using different
colours or point styles to differentiate between them.
Line graphs are most commonly used for changes over time.
Labelling graphs
It is essential to label graphs properly; otherwise anyone
using them will not be able to get all the information
from them. You should label axes and provide a key to the
lines or bars.
```

Activity 6

1 Load up the file **UNIT21-2**, if it is not already on screen
2 Set paper size to A5 portrait (*see* Unit 12), making sure to change initial codes, as well as page layout. Set top margin to 0.75" and bottom margin to 0.5"
3 Define a two column layout, with margins of 0.5" at each side and 0.5" between the columns *(Measurements: 0.5",2.66";3.16",5.33"* for positions of each side of each column)
4 Exit to the text and preview to check the display. Reveal codes to check your column definition
5 Save the file before continuing
6 Set up 3 styles called Side heading, Sub heading and Main title as follows:
Side heading - Sans Serif 10 cpi/Helvetica 12 pt, bold, left justified
Sub heading - Sans Serif 7 cpi/Helvetica 14 pt, bold, centred
Main title - Sans Serif 5 cpi/Helvetica 18 pt, bold, centred
7 Set up the initial codes to give the Base font Roman 12 cpi orTimes Roman 10 point, fully justified
8 Apply the style Side heading to each of the headings *Pie chart*, *Bar chart*, etc, as shown in the example and insert a blank line before each of them
9 Define a **G**raphics **F**igure with no borders and zero margins
10 Save the file before continuing
11 Create a graphics box with the following specifications

OPTION	SETTING
Position	At the top margin, ie 0.75" vertically from the top of the page; Across the page, ie 0.5" from left margin, 4.83" long
Text	Graphics drawing programs
Style	Main title

12 Add a horizontal ruling line with the following specifications:

OPTION	SETTING
Position	Above the top margin, ie 0.65" vertically from the top of the page Across the page ie, 0.5" from left margin, 4.83" long
Width	0.08" ie very thick

13 Add three more graphics boxes in the positions indicated in the example with the following specifications:

OPTION	SETTING
Position	At the first line of text after the box [*move cursor first*]
Size	1 column wide, ie 2.16" by 0.15" high
Text	1 Capabilities 2 Applications 3 Choosing graph styles
Style	Sub heading

14 Add a vertical line between columns width 0.02", set at 1.25" from the top and 6.52" long
15 Save, preview and print

Graphics drawing programs

Capabilities

Most drawing programs are capable of the following: text in several sizes, weights and styles; simple shapes, such as rectangles, circles and arcs; lines of different thicknesses at any angle and shading in various weights or patterns.

The program may be a separate package or part of a more comprehensive package, such as Desk Top Publishing.

Applications

There are a number of ways in which drawing packages can be used, producing simple diagrams; positioning large text on a page and for simple drawings.

Choosing graphic styles

Pie chart

A single pie chart can be used to present only one set of figures. Each figure is shown as a percentage of the total of all the figures, with the angle of each pie slice representing the percentage. It is only suitable for situations when the total is significant; in any other situation, a pie chart will be inappropriate and will give false information.

Bar chart

A bar chart uses the length of bars of equal width to represent one set of numerical values. It enables comparison between the values in the set, merely by looking at the lengths.

Multiple bar chart

If you have more than one set of figures, and comparisons are to made between sets, as well as between figures in the same set, then multiple bar charts are used. The bars can be stacked, ie the second set on top of the first set, in which case the total of the two sets can also be compared. Alternatively, the bars can be next to each other, in which case shading is used to pick out each set of figures.

Line graph

If you are mainly interested in the change in one or more set of figures, then a line graph may be suitable, where points are plotted and joined with lines, using different colours or point styles to

Further uses

1 Concert programmes

2 Magazines

3 Brochures

Problem solving

- *Your horizontal ruling line is across only the first column, rather than both.*

  You created the line with the cursor after the **[Col On]** code. Reveal codes and delete the line code. Then move your cursor to a position before the code and create the line again.

- *Your horizontal line begins .5" in from the margin, instead of at the margin.*

  You have not set the horizontal position. Move the cursor to highlight the line code and edit it.

- *Your box does not appear on the page when you preview the text.*

  It may be on the next page; press **PgDn** to see the second page to check this. The most likely change needed is that you have chosen an impossible setting for vertical position, so it has been moved to the next page to fit it in. You will need to edit your graphics figure.

- *You have edited your graphics figure, but seem to have had no effect.*

  You may not have chosen the correct Figure number to edit. Check the number of the figure which you want to change, and key it in when asked during the editing process.

- *Your vertical line between columns runs over the main title and/or into the bottom margin*

  You selected **Full Page** for the vertical position of your line, instead of starting it 1.25" from the top of the page and giving it a length of 6.52". Reveal codes and highlight the **[Vline ....]** code. Select **Line** from the **Graphics** menu and choose **Edit Vertical** to display the line's features and change them.

- *The margins you chose for the newspaper columns do not seem to be able to cope with the text. Some text is not shown on screen.*

  You may have forgotten to change the Initial codes when you selected the paper size, so you still have 1" margins, rather than the 0.5" margins required. Use **Layout Document Initial Codes** to change them and preview again.

Function keys

Function keys are set up quite differently in the DOS and Windows versions of WordPerfect 5.1, so they have been used very little in the main text. Instead, the menu options have been suggested.

DOS version

The table below shows what functions or menu selections are accessible through the function keys using the DOS version of WordPerfect 5.1. The function keys can be used on their own or in combination with the Ctrl key, the Shift key or the Alt key.

	KEY ALONE	WITH CTRL	WITH SHIFT	WITH ALT
F1	Edit **U**ndelete	Goto DOS	**F**ile **S**etup	**T**hesaurus
F2	Search **F**orward	Spell	Search **B**ackward	Search **R**eplace
F3	Help	**E**dit **W**indow	**E**dit **S**witch Doc	Reveal Codes
F4	**L**ayout **A**lign **I**ndent	Block operations	**L**ayout **A**lign **I**ndent	**E**dit **B**lock
F5	**F**iles List **F**iles	**F**ile Text **I**n/**O**ut	**T**ools	Mark
F6	Bold	**L**ayout **A**lign **T**ab	Centre	Flush Right
F7	Exit	**L**ayout **F**ootnote	Print	**L**ayout **C**olumns
F8	Underline	F**o**nt	Layout menu	**L**ayout **S**tyles
F9	{End Field}	**T**ools **M**erge	**T**ools Merge Codes	**G**raphics
F10	**F**ile **S**ave	**T**ools **M**acro **D**efine	**F**ile **R**etrieve	**T**ools **M**acro **E**xecute
F11	Reveal Codes			

Windows

Function key use is not recommended with the Windows version of WordPerfect, as most functions are accessible much more quickly through the menus. However, for completeness, the table below shows the Windows function key uses.

	KEY ALONE	WITH CTRL	WITH SHIFT	WITH ALT
F1	Help	Speller	What is?	Thesaurus
F2	Search		Search Next	Search Previous
F3	Save as	Screen	Save	Reveal Codes
F4	Open	Close Doc.	New	Close App.
F5	Print	Date Text	Print Preview	Para. Number
F6	Next Pane	Next Doc.	Previous Pane	Next Window
F7	Exit	Hanging Indent	Centre	Flush Right
F8	Select	Margins	Select Cell	Styles
F9	Font	Tables	Line Layout	Page Layout
F10	Menu	Macro Record		Macro Play
F11	Open Figure	Horiz. Line	Edit Figure	Text Box
F12		Merge	Mark Text	Tools Define

Glossary

Align	To place text in a straight line, either to the left or to the right
Block	A piece of text which has been marked by selecting Block from the Edit menu or by using the mouse to be moved or copied
Backspace delete	Key which deletes the character to the left of the cursor
Calculations	A simple facility within tables, selected by choosing Maths
Centring	Positioning text centrally on a line or on the page
Control Printer	Screen which displays the progress of any printing you are carrying out
Cursor	A flashing video block marking the point where text is entered
Cut and paste	Remove blocks of text or move them to a new position
Date code	Menu option allowing the current date to be inserted into your document
Default	Any pre-set value, for margins, tabs, paper size, printer, font, alignment or any other feature
Delete	Key which deletes the character at the cursor position
Editing	Making changes by deleting, inserting or moving text
Edit menu	Menu containing all editing and movement options
Embolden	Text which is overstruck to give a darker, thicker effect
Ending pages	Using **Ctrl Return** to end a page before the default position
Enhancement	Emboldening, underlining, italics and other effects used to highlight or enhance text

Field	An item of data contained in a record
File menu	Menu for file, printing and setup operations
Font	A style of print. A font list is given in the Font menu
Font menu	Menu containing all font and appearance options
Footer	A line of text which appears on all or alternate pages containing file names and page numbers
Footnote	An addition to an item in the text, placed at the bottom of the appropriate page, or the end of the document.
Format	The layout of a document or file
Formulae	Mathematical computations in tables
Global replace	Replacement of text which is carried out automatically for every occurrence of the text
Graphics boxes	A method of boxing text, pictures and equations
Graphics menu	Menu which gives access to all graphics boxes and lines
Hard copy	A paper copy of the work on screen
Header	A line of text appearing on all or alternate pages
Highlight	Reverse video shading, or colour, which can help you to identify text to be changed or moved
Horizontal centring	Work centred across a page
Indent	Text inset from the main body of the work
Initial Codes	The default codes for a document
Inserting rows/cols	Adding rows and columns to a table
Insert mode	Keying text inserts it before the existing text
Justify	Text with an even left or right margin
Joining/splitting cells	The Tables facility which allows cell manipulation
Layout menu	Menu containing all formatting options
List files	A command giving a display of the files on disk
Macro	Standard words or phrases composed by selecting Macro from the Tools menu, followed by Define
Mailmerge	Merging 2 files to produce a personalised letter
Move (cut)	A function to move or cut text through the Edit menu

On line	An active operation, particularly an active printer
Outlining	A system of numbering automatically
Pagination	This is the way in which pages are organised and numbere
Page break	Ending a page at a specified point
Paper type	A set size and type of paper used for printing
Paste	Place text which has been cut in a new position
Preview	Inspect the layout of your document before printing
Printer screen	Screen which presents all the printing alternatives
Record	Data stored for reference purposes
Remove lines	Lines can be removed from a table
Retrieve	Recall a file from disk for editing or subsequent use
Reveal codes	Show on screen, along with your text, the invisible codes wihich set display and format for the text
Right align	Line text up to the right margin, or to a set point on the page
Ruling lines	Horizontal and vertical lines used to emphasise text or items
Selective replace	Replacement of text which has to be confirmed for every occurrence of the text
Setup	Menu option which lets you choose display, editing, hardware and menu options
Spell check	Looking up words in a disk-based dictionary to find and correct spelling and typing mistakes
Style	A set of features specifying the appearance of text
Subscript	Smaller lowered character
Superscript	Smaller raised characters
Tab key	Key providing automatic stops for text insertion at intervals
Table	A method of displaying text in columns and rows, which can be used in preference to tab settings
Template	File containing a standard document, which can be used to produce this sort of document
Text size	The text sizes you can use depend on the printer you are using. To view the sizes available, print out the file PRINTER.TST
Thesaurus	A method of looking up alternative words

Tools menu	Menu containing special options, eg spellcheck, Thesaurus, macros, mailmerge
Typing screen	The screen that you see; it usually contains 22 lines
Undelete	If you have deleted a line and then changed your mind, you may undelete through the Edit menu
Underline	One of the ways in which the appearance of text can be altered, found in the Font menu, or using key **F8**
Vertical centring	Work centred down a page

Index